The Connection Between Childhood Trauma and Substance Abuse

Heal from the Emotions to Overcome the Addiction

Evie Wright

contained within this document, including, but not limited to, errors, omissions, or inaccuracies.

Table of Contents

Introduction

I have absolutely no pleasure in the stimulants in which I sometimes so madly indulge. It has not been in the pursuit of pleasure that I have periled life and reputation and reason. It has been in the desperate attempt to escape from torturing memories . . . from a sense of insupportable loneliness and a dread of some strange impending doom. –From the letters of Edgar Allan Poe

This quote by one of the most popular authors to this day, Edgar Allan Poe, is proof that even the most famous and the most successful people can suffer from both trauma and substance abuse. These conditions did not stand in the way of him having a successful life, but they did make it more difficult. Just like Poe, who was able to use his experiences to give deeper meaning and poignancy to his art, people can grow from their experiences into stronger individuals. Especially, since you have something that Poe did not, this book to help you get through the hard times and move on with a healthy, more fulfilling life.

The pain and problems that you face from your trauma are understandable, and your feelings are completely valid. It is a common occurrence that people who suffered unimaginable trauma often blame themselves, or feel like they could have put a stop to what happened to them. That is not always the case. Nobody has the right to hurt you or get upset with you because you can't just "move on." That is a phrase that many trauma survivors hear throughout their life, "It's in the past. Why can't you just move on and get over it?" But how can you move on healthily without the right tools and skills? How do you move forward if you were never taught how to express your feelings properly?

Luckily, you have made a step in the right direction. With the resources and examples provided in this book, you can learn how strong the link is between exposure to childhood trauma and substance abuse, how to replace your unsafe behaviors with healthier ones, learn the early signs or established symptoms of a deep-rooted problem, and how to spot a build-up of symptoms pushing you toward a potential relapse.

Chapter 1:

What Is Childhood Trauma?

The greater a child's terror, and the earlier it is experienced, the harder it becomes to develop a strong and healthy sense of self. –Nathaniel Branden

What Is Trauma?

Trauma doesn't discriminate, as it can happen to any gender, at any age, and under any circumstances. The people that are assaulted or abused experience trauma, but so do the ones that see these violent acts first-hand. However, assault and abuse are not the only incidents that can cause trauma. Unexpected tragedies such as the death of a loved one, car accidents, and natural disasters can bring about the same results. Children lack the emotional capability of coping with traumatic events and are found to be extremely susceptible to the aftermath due to the inability to properly recover. Substance abuse is often a big part of that aftermath, giving reason to believe that more people are dealing with unresolved childhood trauma than we previously thought.

Any event that a child would consider dangerous, frightening, or threatening to their life would be considered a traumatic event. Witnessing the same type of events happen to a loved family member, like a parent or sibling, can give the same result. The removal of their safety, or the person that they depend on to keep them safe, can have negative physical and emotional implications for years after the event. The child can be left to feel mentally and emotionally hopeless and frequently afraid, while physically feeling nauseous, a pounding heart, and lose control over their bladder and bowels. These lingering manifestations can cause them to feel extremely overwhelmed as they deal with the fact that they were unable to protect themselves or that anyone was able to stop the event from happening. Even though parents and other adults in an authoritative position, like teachers, do their best to protect children, accidents and tragedies can still happen.

What Can Trauma Look Like?

Whenever a person experiences something that threatens their life or safety, is physically injured, or witnesses someone go through these things, what they are experiencing can accurately be described as trauma. How the person deals with their reaction to this traumatic event varies depending on their resilience. Adults can be traumatized as well; however, their previous experiences and advanced mental capacities make it easier for them to cope compared to young children. Sometimes these feelings surrounding the trauma or tragic accidents remain unresolved, and what could have been short-term problems turn into serious long-term issues. One of these serious long-term issues is post-traumatic stress disorder (PTSD), which can play a major role in disrupting one's emotional, mental, physical, and social wellbeing.

Trauma can be broken down into three main categories: acute, chronic, and complex. Acute trauma is characterized as trauma caused by one particular event, such as a serious car accident or being assaulted by a stranger. Trauma that happens repeatedly over a long span of time, like witnessing or being the victim of domestic abuse, is considered to be chronic trauma. A combination of being exposed to multiple and varying types of trauma is known as complex trauma.

Types of Traumatic Events

The types of traumatic events that fall into these three categories can range from natural events, like hurricanes, to medical illnesses to multiple types of abuse. School violence, domestic terrorism, kidnapping, or the unexpected loss of a loved one is considered to be acute trauma. Even though the word 'acute' may give the impression that the trauma may not be as significant as others, these are examples of this category because they are usually a one-time occurrence. Physical, mental, and sexual abuse, including human trafficking, fall into the category of chronic trauma. Extreme neglect and being deprived of essential needs also fall into this category. Examples of complex trauma would include stressors related to the military, such as the frequent deployment of a parent, and a family member's substance abuse problem or emotional neglect.

What is Child Traumatic Stress?

Child traumatic stress is described as the suffering of a child due to one or more traumatic events and the adverse reactions to those traumas affect all parts of their daily lives. These reactions can affect their ability to regulate their emotions, cause depression and severe anxiety, academic and work-related problems, avoiding emotional and physical attachments with others, difficulty falling and staying asleep, nightmares when they do fall asleep, regression in their age-appropriate skills, and noticeable changes in their behavior. When children are reminded of these traumas they can exhibit these reactions as well.

Older children may show their adverse reactions in other ways. They may use drugs or alcohol as a way to cope. Preteens and teenagers might start to make risky and impulsive decisions, including breaking the law and engaging in unprotected sexual activities with multiple partners. Age is not a discriminatory factor when it comes to a child's immunity to trauma. Infants and toddlers can experience trauma, but how they react later in life to that trauma will depend on their level of development.

Early Childhood Trauma

A child that is dealing with the daily stresses of overcoming trauma may present their reactions in many ways. Certain stimuli can cause different reactions, especially sensory stimuli. Loud noises or crashes, sudden and violent movements, and things that they see visually as frightening can create a feeling of losing their sense of safety. The scary images of their traumas that they see reenacted in front of them by television shows and movies can also show up in their dreams. Children's brains are unable to tell the truth from what is seen in their nightmares, and can often create new fears.

A child's vulnerability puts them at a major risk of being exposed to trauma. Not only are they less likely to think of the possibilities of dangerous situations and their ability to protect themselves, but they tend to find a way to blame themselves for anything bad that does happen. The reason for this vulnerability in children is the developing cerebral cortex in their brain—an area in the brain that controls their memories, attention span, thinking and language skills, planning and organization, and consciousness. The damage done by childhood trauma can have a severe impact on their IQ, the ability to regulate their emotions, and feel safe. As a result, they may go out of their way to avoid attachments to other people. Without these attachments to their parents or other caregivers, the child will become extremely stressed and start to display behaviors that are out of character for them. These newly developed behaviors confuse their caregivers, making it difficult to figure out how to deal with the child and makes the ability to connect even more challenging.

Symptoms and Behaviors for Children Ages 0–2

Children that have been exposed to trauma at this young age can demonstrate their symptoms in many ways. Some children may be clingy in new situations, while others can seem aggressive and avoidant. Babies and toddlers under the age of three can show signs of a decreased appetite, problems with their digestive system, and slow weight gain or rapid weight loss. They can demonstrate a problem with retaining new information, making and maintaining eye contact, and have trouble communicating verbally. These children will scream or cry excessively, and are difficult to soothe. They may take on a look of being frozen in fear or appear to be cut off from their emotions. Children at this age can regress on the milestones that they have already accomplished, like walking, crawling, and sitting up on their own. Removing traumatized children in this age group from their primary caregiver can create a highly distressing situation for them, even if the parent is only gone for a very short time.

Symptoms and Behaviors for Children Ages 3–6

This age group comes with its own set of symptoms and behaviors. Children between the ages of three to six that have been exposed to trauma can develop learning disabilities, creating focusing and learning issues in school. These children often act out when they are placed in a social situation, becoming highly aggressive with others and imitating the verbal and physical abuse that they have observed. Their lack of social skills and low level of self-confidence makes it difficult to make new friends or know whom they can trust. Their daily stressors and worries often lead to frequent visits to the school nurse with complaints of headaches and stomachaches.

Reminders and Adversities

Difficult changes are set in motion for children that are exposed to trauma. They could be dealing with moving to a new house, going to new schools, changes in their established routines, and who they are or aren't living with. Some children have to deal with ongoing criminal charges or investigations involving their parents and Child Protective Services. The changes in their daily lives and memories of their experiences serve as a reminder that could eventually become a legacy. The reminders of certain dates, people, emotions, and situations bring about negative behaviors and distressing emotions. If the trauma is not addressed and properly dealt with, the child's ability to recover is significantly compromised; subsequently, this creates bigger problems and severe behavioral issues as they grow older.

Risk and Protective Factors

Just because a child experiences trauma, doesn't mean that they will necessarily develop traumatic stress or the symptoms later on in life. Many contributing factors can reverse the symptoms and adverse effects of trauma, these factors include

- How severe the event was and if the child was directly involved.

- Where the child was when the event occurred and if they witnessed the event or learned of what happened another way (family members telling them about it or seeing it on television).

- How their caregivers reacted when they learned of the trauma and if their admission was taken seriously.

- If the child was exposed to, or a victim of, traumatic events on multiple occasions.

- How the community and their family's culture contribute to the resources and quality of the recovery process in efforts to reduce the symptoms of traumatic stress.

-

Chapter 2:

The Connection Between Childhood Trauma and Substance Abuse

Addiction is not a choice that anybody makes; it's not a moral failure. What it actually is: it's a response to human suffering. —Gabor Maté

Trauma and Brain Development in Children

An immense amount of research has been done with the main purpose of discovering how trauma affects the development of a child's brain. When the child experiences what is considered to be a traumatic event, the body activates and releases hormones that leave the brain at a heightened state of fear and stress for a short time. If the trauma is recurring, or what was discussed previously as chronic trauma, the brain will remain altered at this heightened state. When the brain is consistently in this heightened state of fear and stress, the changes in their cognitive, behavioral, and emotional functioning start to diminish and are replaced with skills that they need in order to survive. The constant state of being in survival mode impacts the child's physical and mental wellbeing, behavior, and emotional development as they transition into adulthood.

Poor Quality of Life in Adulthood Due to Childhood Trauma

The deeply rooted symptoms of childhood trauma often affect a wide range of areas and severely impact the quality of life well into adulthood. As adults, adversity and troubles in the workplace are common struggles. How they process and perceive the required adversity and the inability to trust their coworkers often lead to difficulties staying with the same job or company for long periods. Their ability to handle all of the responsibilities of their position while struggling to relate to others can significantly impact their quality of life and ability to stay employed.

Survivors of childhood trauma that experienced or witnessed all types of abuse in the home, especially sexual abuse, are likely to experience severe issues when it comes to intimacy and maintaining a healthy relationship. Questioning their sexual identity, discovering their self-worth, and the ability to trust and become assertive with their partner are all shown to be common obstacles when an adult with unresolved trauma starts to date. Having issues with avoiding unhealthy or abusive relationships and the red flags that are presented at the beginning of the relationship can lead them into other traumatic situations, causing further damage to their quality of life.

Multiple psychological illnesses can be brought on by abuse and trauma experienced during childhood, eating disorders being one of the most reported. According to a study done by the New York Center for Eating Disorders, almost 50% of the patients that are seen and treated for eating disorders were at one point a victim of sexual abuse during their childhood (Silver Mist Recovery, 2018). Unlike other people, in their disordered minds, food doesn't betray them or hurt them. They gain a sense of control over what goes into and out of their body, unlike the trauma they endured during their younger years. Food is one of the most accessible and cheapest ways to alter one's mood, and most patients seeking treatment frequently binged, purged, or starved themselves as children to deal with the emotions surrounding their trauma. The patients report that they fall in love with the sense of control, and this obsession follows them into adulthood.

Prevalence of Addiction in Adults With Childhood Trauma

Eating disorders and food addiction aren't the only prevalent mental illnesses that follow a traumatized child well into adulthood. A child's vulnerability to becoming abused extends to their vulnerability in the use of drugs and alcohol as a way of coping with their emotions. At least 60% of people that abuse these substances reported being either sexually or physically abused in their childhood home (Lesser, 2021). A child experiencing any type of trauma puts them at a higher risk of developing an addiction to mind-altering substances. According to the 2000 study, "Childhood Trauma As a Correlate Lifetime Opiate Use in Psychiatric Patients," done by the Cornell University Medical Center states that in the cases of 763 admitted inpatient psychiatric patients there was a strong relationship between opiate use and childhood abuse. The study also reported that the use of opiates was 2.7 times more likely in adults with a history of sexual or physical abuse than the patients that were not opiate users. Cornell University Medical Center states in the study that, "opiate use was higher among those reporting physical abuse alone (24.1%) or physical and sexual abuse (27%) than among those reporting sexual abuse alone (8.8%)" (Heffernan et al., 2000).

Researchers have worked on multiple studies in an attempt to connect how trauma and abuse are frequently linked, and why so many people that have had a traumatic event in their lives turn to drugs and alcohol in order to cope. Data collected during a study done by the Kaiser Permanente's Adverse Childhood Experiences indicates that in over 17,000 of their patients "a child who experiences four or more traumatic events is five times more likely to become an alcoholic, 60% more likely to become obese, and up to 46 times more likely to become an injection-drug user than the general population" (Hackensack Meridian Carrier Clinic, 2019).

As stated earlier, child abuse isn't the only traumatic event that results in vulnerability to addictive behaviors. Other trauma-inducing events such as severe neglect, losing their parent or caregiver unexpectedly, witnessing abuse in the home, and having a family member in the home suffering from a mental illness can create a predisposition to substance abuse. Their predisposal and addictions don't always have to include illegal substances or alcohol. Sometimes their addiction can be behavior-based, such as compulsive sexual activity or compulsive eating.

Correlations Between the Types of Child Abuse and Types of Addiction

Certain types of abuse are often connected to the use of particular addictions within the traumatized population as means of coping. According to a study done by the National Institute of Mental Health in 2010, various substances (44.8% marijuana, 6.2% heroin and opiates, 34.1% cocaine, and 39% alcohol) were found to be used at extremely high rates amongst this group. Particularly, the use of cocaine is found to be predominantly used amongst those that experienced emotional, sexual, and physical abuse as a child (Khoury et al., 2010). It is also used to deal with the daily PTSD symptoms that customarily occur with these types of interpersonal traumas.

Reasons Behind the Link Between Childhood Trauma and Addiction

There are reasons that the co-occurrence of trauma and addictions often merge in one person. One main reason is that turning to drugs and alcohol as a way to self-medicate makes someone that has failed to manage the effects of trauma feel that they can do so. Self-medicating on their own terms makes their life and symptoms manageable, even if it is destructive to their health.

People that use alcohol or drugs to self-medicate would rather feel the sedative or stimulating qualities of the substance than symptoms that are exhibited in PTSD. Feeling numb or high seems better to them than feeling easily frightened by sudden movements and loud noises, agitated, socially withdrawn, depressed, or plagued with insomnia. Unfortunately, the self-medicating stops becoming a cure for their symptoms, and starts to become a problem on its own, therefore creating another hurdle or obstacle that they will have to get over in order to recover.

A lifestyle filled with substance abuse doesn't necessarily help the traumatized stay safe, but can put them in more danger. Being in dangerous neighborhoods and around unpredictable people that abuse drugs make someone more of a target than someone that does not participate in this type of risky behavior. Driving while impaired or being the passenger of an impaired driver puts a substance abuser at risk of being injured or killed in a car accident. Alcohol and drug abuse also make one susceptible to violence and abuse than someone who has not been predisposed to these traumatic acts earlier in life. There could also be a genetic component that links addictive tendencies with people that are more likely to have PTSD, but research hasn't gone far enough to make a reasonable and scientific conclusion on this finding yet.

Trauma Can Hide Behind Substance Abuse

For a while, self-medicating with drugs and alcohol may seem like it helps with the flashbacks and the recurrent memories of trauma. The memories start to go away, so it seems like that the recovery from substance abuse and other addictions are the only issues that they have to deal with. Ignoring the trauma that they have suppressed for so long may make them work harder to get sober and stay that way, but more often than not, the addictive behavior is channeled into other addictions. The person avoiding the possibility of recovering from their trauma may be able to stay away from drugs, but they may start compulsively eating, gambling, and shopping. Compulsive behavior, like sexual promiscuity, is going to continue their suffering until their trauma is resolved.

Dealing with unresolved childhood trauma is a hard task to accomplish without the use of mind-altering substances, but using and abusing these types of substances makes it nearly impossible. Therapists will most likely recommend that someone who is struggling with a traumatic past and substance abuse problems deal with their addiction first. A person with a history of trauma cannot resolve their feelings about what happened if their mind isn't clear and they can't think rationally. They are unable to connect how their usage of alcohol and drugs is part of a bigger underlying issue. Something that started as a way to cope and suppress their memories, took over their entire life until they couldn't see what the original problem was anymore.

Once the person can think rationally and clearly without the use of substances in their system, they can start working in individual or group therapy sessions to deal with the underlying issue. Treatments have been created specifically for people dealing with the effects of trauma and PTSD. These treatments include: PTSD interventions, therapy focused specifically on the trauma and learning new coping skills, and medications to help with co-occurring mental illnesses like depression and anxiety. If someone is dealing with the comorbid symptoms of trauma and substance abuse, speaking with a trained therapist can open many doors by addressing the correct issues and creating an individualized treatment plan.

Chapter 3:

Being Trauma-Informed

As discussed previously, acute trauma is caused by an event that occurs rarely but leaves a lasting effect. If these effects last longer than a span of three days to a month and are not resolved through therapy or other means, the symptoms may magnify and turn into PTSD.

Post-Traumatic Stress Disorder: Do you have it?

Post-traumatic stress disorder symptoms vary from person to person. Emotions ranging from fear to hopelessness may be experienced by one person, while others may experience severe dissociative symptoms, such as derealization and depersonalization. Take a minute of your time and ask yourself a few questions.

- Did you experience or witness a traumatic event?

- Do you experience recurrent and intrusive memories about the event?

- Have you experienced persistent distressing dreams at night surrounding the traumatic events?

- Have you experienced dissociative symptoms, like flashbacks, that cause you to feel like the trauma is happening again?

- Have your flashbacks caused you to lose awareness of what is happening in your present surroundings?

- Do you experience an emotional or physical response when you are internally and externally triggered by a reminder of or a resemblance to the event(s)?

- Do you make an effort to avoid all memories, feelings, and reminders, including people or locations, of the traumatic event?

- Do you find large periods missing (before, during, and after) in regard to memories surrounding the event(s)?

- Do you experience constant exaggerated negative beliefs about yourself (feeling as if you are a bad person) and the world (feeling like the world and everyone in it is dangerous)?

- Do you feel as if the world is constantly against you and you cannot trust others?

- Do you blame yourself for the event happening, or your inability to stop it from occurring?

- Are you stuck in a repetitive negative emotional state, such as fear, anger, and guilt?

- Do you feel a minimized interest in the activities or hobbies that you once enjoyed?

- Do you feel an estrangement or detachment from other people, even with others not associated with the trauma?

- Do you feel like you are unable to feel positive emotions, like happiness, love, or pride?

- Are you frequently in an irritable mood or have angry outbursts with little to no provocation? Or are you expressing physical or verbal aggression toward others?

- Are you exhibiting unusual reckless and impulsive self-destructive behavior?

- Do you find yourself in a continuous hypervigilant state or always feel on the edge of your seat?

- Do you have trouble concentrating at work and retaining information?

- Do you have an issue falling or staying asleep, or feel like you are restless when you lay down at night?

If you answered 'yes' to many of these questions, and have been dealing with these symptoms for over a month, you may be exhibiting the signs and symptoms of post-traumatic stress disorder. Speaking to a therapist to resolve your emotional and mental connection to the trauma you experienced can help remarkably. Unresolved trauma and PTSD can lead to major impairments in all areas of your life, including your occupational and social life.

Post-Traumatic Stress Disorder for Children Six Years and Younger

Children ages six years and younger that have been exposed to a threat to their safety or a serious injury or violence within the home can experience their own set of symptoms, differentiating from that of adults. If you (when thinking back on your childhood) or your child, answer yes to some of these questions, the red flags of PTSD may have already taken hold.

- Did you, or your child, experience or witness a traumatic event before the age of six?

- Did you, or your child, experience recurrent and intrusive memories about the event shortly after it occurred?

- Did you, or your child, experience persistent distressing dreams at night surrounding the traumatic events? Are the frightening feelings after you, or your child, wake up related to the event?

- Was the content of your, or your child's, dreams related to the trauma or event(s)?

- Have you, or your child, re-enacted the trauma during playtime with toys or others?

- Did you, or your child, experience dissociative symptoms, like flashbacks, that cause you, or them, to feel like the trauma is happening again?

- Did you, or your child, make an effort to avoid all memories, feelings, and reminders, including people or locations, of the traumatic event starting at a young age?

- Did you, or your child, avoid conversations that could possibly bring up unwanted memories or feelings about the event?

- Do you remember feeling stuck in a repetitive negative emotional state, such as fear, anger, and guilt?

- Did you, or your child, suddenly lose interest in the activities or hobbies that you, or they, previously enjoyed, including the interest in playing?

- Did you, or your child, slowly withdraw from socializing with other children and adults?

- Did you, or your child, feel like you are unable to feel positive emotions, like happiness, love, or pride?

- Did you, or your child, show physical and verbal aggression toward others without being provoked?

- Did you, or your child, start having extreme temper tantrums that were out of the ordinary?

- Did you, or your child, find yourself to be in a continuous hypervigilant state or always feel on the edge of your seat even at a young age?

- Did you, or your child, get frightened easily, like an exaggerated response to sudden movements?

- Did you, or your child, have trouble concentrating at school and have difficulty retaining newly learned information?

- Did you, or your child, have an issue falling or staying asleep, or feeling restless when you lay down at night?

- Did you, or your child, frequently wet the bed after being fully potty trained?

What Does Trauma Do To You?

The development of these symptoms is considered to be the essential feature in the criteria of PTSD. Their behavioral and emotional symptoms tend to dominate their lives, and their dysphoric and negative moods cause a major amount of distress. Some people experience dissociative and reactive symptoms when they are exposed to a trigger that reminds them of their trauma. However, an individual can have a combination of these symptoms.

Symptoms of dissociative issues can include derealization and depersonalization. Depersonalization is described as the feeling you have when you are detached from the world around you. Some people describe it as feeling outside of their bodies or watching themselves from across the room. Derealization is described as the feeling you get when you feel as if you are living in a dream state. Some people may describe it as feeling like they are living in a movie, and nothing seems real to them. Both of these dissociative issues are considered to be a major indicator of PTSD if they occur persistently.

What Is a Traumatizing Event for Adults and Children?

What is considered to be traumatic to people varies, just as the symptoms of PTSD and trauma-related reactions do. Events such as a lifelong or chronic illness are not considered traumatic events; however, catastrophic events like anaphylactic shock can be considered traumatic because the onset is usually unexpected and sudden.

Traumatic events that can affect adults include

- Directly experiencing a threat to their safety or the actual act of physical violence. For example: a sexual assault, mugging, childhood abuse (physical, emotional, mental, and/or sexual), being kidnapped, or a hostage situation.

- Being exposed to the violence of war and combat, whether as a soldier or a civilian. For example: being tortured, being incarcerated as a prisoner of war, or experiencing a terrorist attack.

- The threat of or actual act of sexual violence. For example: a violent or forceful sexual assault, date rape occurring more often with the use of drugs and alcohol, being a victim of sex trafficking, or nonconsensual contact.

- Natural and man-made disasters.

- Serious injury due to car accidents.

- Witnessing a traumatic event first-hand. For example: seeing someone being assaulted or threatened, an unnatural and/or violent death, a violent assault (physical or sexual assault), or seeing their child injured medically (losing a limb, knocked unconscious).

- Learning about a traumatic event through indirect exposure about a close friend of a family member. For example: suicide, drug overdose, violent assault (physical or sexual), or a serious injury (often needing urgent medical attention).

Children can directly experience many of these traumatic events, including witnessing the casualties of war and being forced to become child soldiers in some countries. Sexual abuse doesn't always have to include physical violence when it comes to children, but is rather defined to be sexual contact that is determined to be inappropriate developmentally toward the child. Since children are often listening to their parents more than adults believe, they hear about traumatic events indirectly and often face the issue of dealing with them internally. However, the severity of PTSD and how long the symptoms last usually depend on how intentional the act was and how much they dealt with it personally. The stressor of witnessing a traumatic event is going to be less likely to affect a person's everyday life than being tortured or physically assaulted.

Re-Experiencing the Traumatic Event

A traumatic event, like the ones listed above, can be reexperienced in so many ways. The person dealing with the aftermath of the trauma can find the recurrent recollections of what happened to be intrusive and involuntary in their daily thoughts. The intrusions on their daily thoughts can slowly turn into depressive symptoms and are pushed further along when the memories of the trauma are emphasized by their olfactory or other senses. The components of emotional and physiological behaviors can also emphasize how often these memories intrude on their thoughts. The intrusive re-experiencing of this event can find a way to manifest in one's dreams. The dreams are found to be distressing, with the event replaying or symbolizing the threat of their safety.

It is not uncommon for an individual that is re-experiencing a traumatic event to go into a dissociative episode, sometimes lasting from a few hours to several days. The brain feels as if it has shut down while the individual relives the event so vividly that they lose all grasp on reality. Shortened dissociative episodes are known as flashbacks, and occur with the feelings of distress, hypervigilance, and heightened arousal of their senses. Flashbacks can be triggered by an emotion resembling how they felt during the event or seeing someone that resembles the person that hurt them.

Children re-experience their trauma in various ways. Sometimes the way that they tell what is happening behind closed doors gives outsiders an idea of what they are going through. The ways that a child may re-experience traumatic events include

- Re-enactment through play (with toys or other children).

- Dissociative episodes.

- Rapid heartbeat.

- Uncontrollable sweating.

- Becoming agitated or hypervigilant.

- Visibly upset and unable to be comforted.

- The feeling of "butterflies" in their stomach, or nausea.

- Nightmares, coupled with frequent bedwetting.

Avoiding Stimuli

Once a person has dealt with trauma and the mental, emotional, and physiological effects that the memories bring with it, they will learn what stimuli create these undesired effects subsequently causing them to go out of their way to avoid them. They will deliberately avoid anything that stimulates these memories, including avoiding people, locations, conversations, and feelings. One may create and use other ways to distract themselves in order to avoid the stimuli, such as painting, exercising, or participating in a hobby. They may avoid activities and situations that include stimuli causing them to recollect the event. For example, if a woman is unexpectedly and viciously attacked by a dog while she is taking a walk, she will deliberately avoid the street where the attack occurred due to the anxiety that the memories cause.

Chapter 4:

Understanding How Past Trauma

Shapes Our Reactions

It is hard to break the cycle of victimization and reenactment if the survivor comes from a dysfunctional family not equipped to deal with her plight, if she does not have access to financial or educational resources that could empower her, or if she belongs to a culture that blames her." –Shaili Jain, M.D.

Negative Changes in Thinking and Mood

The way that the brain processes information and one's mood can be negatively altered after a traumatic event occurs. These changes to the brain can manifest themselves in many ways. Some individuals are unable to recall particular parts surrounding the trauma. Someone that thought positively about themselves or was confident before the event, may start making exaggerated and persistent negative comments about themselves and others. For example, they may start questioning their ability to make sound judgments, but before the trauma, they were confident in their choices. Someone whose perception has been changed by an intentional or malicious act will understandably start to question other people's intentions, motives, and trustworthiness.

Post-traumatic stress disorder brings along the blessing of never-ending guilt and self-deprecation. The cognitive changes create the belief that the victim is to blame for what happened to them. This negative mindset will lead to a negative mood, causing one to be stuck in a persistent cycle of anger, fear, or sadness. They may feel less interested or avoid participating in the activities or hobbies they once enjoyed. An individual dealing with PTSD often feels detached from other people and from the ability to feel positive emotions. They feel the need to isolate themselves because they can't be happy and their unhappiness is a burden on everyone around them.

When characterized, PTSD is expressed as the increased feeling of sensitivity to the possibility of threats, especially ones that are related to the traumatic event that one has experienced. For example, if you are in a serious car accident that resulted in severe injury, you may feel on edge when riding in a car. The increased sensitivity can also be heightened during events that aren't related to the trauma, such as a sudden heart attack or medical catastrophe.

Post-traumatic stress disorders are physically displayed by being jumpy, or easily startled when they hear an unexpected loud noise or another person makes sudden movements around them. They may also have issues centered around concentration, like remembering the events of their daily lives, the ability to follow a conversation or focus on tasks in front of them. PTSD can bring the onset of feeling detached from the world around them, along with other dissociative symptoms.

Other Conditions Trauma Can Cause in Adults and Children

Many other conditions can be stressors due to experiencing or witnessing a traumatic event. Adults and children alike can experience a regression in their development. Children can regress in the form of losing their ability to speak properly, or the loss of control of their bladder and bowels is common after experiencing prolonged trauma. Adults regress differently. For example, when an adult that experienced unresolved childhood trauma is around the people, or person, that caused the trauma, they may regress to how they behaved at that specific age. Regression is provoked or triggered by feelings of fear, insecurity, or anxiety causing the traumatized person to backslide to an age where they felt safe.

Reactive Attachment Disorder (RAD) is a common trauma-related response when someone, usually a child, is unable to form a stable relationship and attachment to their primary caregivers. This condition is often found in children that have been placed in foster care due to the frequent changing of caretakers and the initial damage caused by their biological parents' lack of ability to provide for their basic needs. These children may exhibit a withdrawal of emotions, inability to be comforted by their caregivers (parents, foster parents, teachers), unable to respond appropriately to other people's emotions, and unprovoked episodes of negative emotions (sadness, fear, anger). RAD is a rare condition among children, but can cause major impairments in their adult life if these issues are not resolved.

Disinhibited Social Engagement Disorder (DSED) is similar to Reactive Attachment Disorder as it stems from the same cause, yet has a completely different set of symptoms. Rather than the person having the complete inability to create an attachment to others, a person with DSED has no fear of strangers and feels a significant link to the stranger immediately. They may give them unsolicited and expensive gifts, or act inappropriately to get attention from the stranger if their attachment is not reciprocated. When a caregiver notices these signs in a child, they should get therapeutic help, as this disorder can pose a significant risk to their own safety and that of others.

Development and Course

Post-traumatic stress disorder can happen to someone of any age. Interestingly, it can even occur in infants. The symptoms usually start to appear about three months after the trauma occurs, but sometimes there can be a slight delay ranging from months to years. How severely the symptoms exhibit themselves or how dominant they are over the individual's life varies from person to person. The timing or duration of the symptoms can vary as well. Some people experience them for as little as three months before the symptoms disappear, while others experience the symptoms for up to 50 years.

The symptoms can reoccur and intensify if there are ongoing stressors or a new event occurs, retraumatizing the person in the process. The development of PTSD can cause a significant decline in their physical health, cognitive thinking, and complete isolation from socialization. Teenagers may become reluctant to participate in age-appropriate developmental milestones, like dating or driving. They may also see themselves in a negative light, believing strongly that they don't fit in with their peers and are unable to fulfill their long-term goals. Going through phases of irritability and reckless behaviors is normal for adolescents, but for older children that are dealing with symptoms of PTSD, these phases can make a negative impact on their future. Their high level of irritability or aggression can destroy relationships with their peers and affect their behavior at school. Reckless and impulsive behaviors can lead them to injure themselves or others and lead to other thrill-seeking or more high-risk behaviors which may result in a criminal record.

If these symptoms are not resolved by the time the teenager moves into adulthood, they may experience fewer, but still severe, symptoms. Adults may not retell their trauma through play or have a persistent negative mood as young children exhibit, due to their ability to mask their emotions and acknowledge their negative thoughts, but they still display their own set of complications. PTSD is displayed in adults through more extensive avoidant behaviors such as ignoring their physical and mental health and suicidal ideation or attempts.

Development of PTSD in the Preschool Age Group

Parents may notice that their young children have had recurrent nightmares, even if the content of the dreams isn't specific to the trauma. Preschoolers are more likely to reenact the events of the trauma through play than older children, often creating interventions or the ability to stop the trauma. On the other end of the spectrum, some children may avoid playing and be unwilling to explore, and even refuse to participate in new activities. Also, unlike older children, they may not appear to be fearful or afraid when they are exposed to trauma and when they re-experience the event. Even without the presentation of fearful reactions, parents may pick up on noticeable changes in the young child's emotions and behaviors. Young children's acknowledgment of how to express their thoughts and manage their emotions is limited, so their only way to express themselves is through a change of moods. When children in this age group experience chronic childhood trauma, such as domestic violence or sexual abuse, it is hard to pinpoint when the onset of symptoms began.

Factors That Change After the Trauma

Factored into the symptoms of PTSD are the temperamental and environmental changes that one publicly displays in their daily life. Temperamental changes include negative judgments about themselves and others, coping mechanisms that are considered inappropriate, and displaying signs of acute stress disorder. Environmental changes include the hyper focus on upsetting reminders surrounding the event, trouble with finances and other losses related to the trauma (such as loss of support system or spouse), and changes in their life leaving them more susceptible to being traumatized again.

Gender-Related Differences

Post-traumatic stress disorder is more likely to be found in females than males. Women, and girls, are also more likely to experience the symptoms of PTSD longer than men do. The high likelihood of women being diagnosed with PTSD is attributed to the fact that they are more likely to be victimized or exposed to trauma sometime during their lives. Females are more likely to become the victims of sexual assault and domestic violence than males. Countries with populations that are exposed to recurrent violent stressors, such as frequent warfare or police states, find that the likelihood of PTSD does not differ between the genders.

Suicide Risk

Experiencing traumatic events can increase the chances of one taking their own life, especially in those that were chronically victimized as children. The emotional reactions associated with PTSD make the chances of suicidal ideation and unsuccessful attempts increase even higher. The mere presence of this trauma-related disorder is an indicator of how likely they are to make a plan to commit suicide and the likelihood that they will go through with their plan.

The overwhelming symptoms cause the person with PTSD so much distress that they start to believe that the only way to get rid of the recurrent memories, anxiety, and anger is to end their lives. Their depressive episodes, lack of a support system, and oftentimes a problem with substance abuse make the risk of suicide or attempts more prevalent.

Functional Consequences

Post-traumatic stress disorder comes with a high-cost margin, whether it's in one's impaired functioning or economic costs. The association of physical, emotional, and social disabilities brings with it an impairment in their physical health and ability to be successful in the workplace. It also costs healthy relationships with their family and peers, a higher income, and chances to be successful in an educational environment. In an economic sense, people with PTSD tend to utilize various medical services at a higher rate, along with social services and government aid.

Trauma in Relation to Other Conditions

The chances of an individual having other mental disorders or illnesses are 80% higher if the individual has PTSD. Among military personnel, about 48% of soldiers injured in combat have a comorbidity of PTSD and a traumatic brain injury, or TBI (American Psychiatric Association, 2017). Children exhibit different comorbid conditions and patterns than adults, sharing at least one other psychiatric diagnosis with PTSD (including separation anxiety and oppositional defiant disorder). Other comorbid mental illnesses include, but are not limited to: bipolar disorder, depression, generalized anxiety disorder, and substance abuse or addiction.

A majority of men and women that seek help for their substance abuse problems, whether it is the use of alcohol or illegal narcotics, report at least one traumatic event occurring before they started using. Most of these events were some form of violence in the home, including physical and sexual abuse. In 2001, the American Journal of Psychiatry stated in their study, "Substance Use Disorder in Patients with Posttraumatic Stress Disorder" (Jacobsen et al., 2001), that:

> High rates of comorbidity suggest that PTSD and substance use disorders are functionally related to one another. Most published data support a pathway whereby PTSD precedes substance abuse or dependence. Substances are initially used to modify PTSD symptoms. With the development of dependence, physiologic arousal resulting from substance withdrawal may exacerbate PTSD symptoms, thereby contributing to a relapse of substance use.

A comorbid substance abuse disorder is more common among men than women. However, as previously stated, women are twice as likely to have PTSD as men. Women are also more likely to abuse opioids, marijuana, cocaine, and sedatives at the same rate to deal with the symptoms. There isn't much of a difference between genders when it comes to the use of alcohol, or alcoholism, as a comorbid condition with PTSD.

Chapter 5:

Trauma-Addiction Across

Childhood

Trauma can seriously affect a person's evolution as they move from childhood into the stages of early adulthood. It disrupts the milestones, challenges, and changes at each temporary stage in their life. The factors that make up these parts of their lives, from physiological to cognitive to socialization, are related to the amount of risk the adolescent faces when it comes to the co-occurrence of PTSD and addiction. While there is a primary focus on the link between post-traumatic stress disorder and the use of illegal substances and alcohol, a profound link between PTSD and the use of tobacco has also been found. Tobacco, or the overall use of nicotine, is found to be used by at least 44% of people that have experienced or been exposed to trauma in their lifetime, especially those exposed to physical abuse or violence within the home (Budenz et al., 2021). Nicotine dependence is associated with the numbing sensation it provides in efforts to avoid the symptoms of PTSD.

Childhood

Take Madison's Story

Madison is a nine-year-old girl at a new school. She often found herself to be the target of cruel jokes and vicious bullying by her classmates. The taunting from her peers eventually escalated to threats of physical violence, and on occasion, physical altercations. Afraid to tell her parents about the bullying and feeling unsafe at school, Madison started to withdraw and started to avoid spending time with the small number of friends she did have out of fear of being attacked. When teachers confronted her about the bullying, she denied any wrongdoing by her classmates due to the belief that her teachers wouldn't believe her. She started to believe that she deserved the cruel treatment of her classmates because she didn't fit in and was seen as 'weird.' Madison's behavior in school has recently become very unusual, and the teachers are starting to take notice. She has begun to act out in class and flies into fits of rage, even when she is unprovoked. Her behavior change confused her parents and teachers because she has always been considered to be a well-behaved child and a good student.

Biological Considerations

Cognitive, emotional, and physical development define the progress through the childhood years, laying the foundation on how to function through the adolescent years in order to move into adulthood. Being exposed to trauma during this stage makes an impact on how their brain processes situations around them and the overall structure of their brain. It creates dysfunction in how the brain responds to emotions, regulating moods, control of cognitive function, impulse control, and responses to stress. This level of dysfunction also increases the child's vulnerability to various psychological issues and negative behaviors that can lead them down a dangerous path, including the use of drugs and alcohol. These brain changes have been linked to the child being involved in risky and reckless behaviors; subsequently, not only increasing their chances of partaking in substance abuse, but their behavior also increases the chance of being exposed to more trauma.

Behavioral and Psychosocial Considerations

Exposure to violence at an early age disrupts the progression of a child's development in their primary years. The effects of the violence manifest themselves as depression, anxiety, and PTSD which only further disrupt their development. The child will internalize and externalize their symptoms, ranging from depression to risky sexual behaviors. The internalizing and externalizing of these symptoms are a known gateway to the path of substance abuse.

Exposure to trauma can also play a drastic role in a child's sense of belonging in the world. It affects their ability to be confident in their relationships with other people, platonic and romantic included. Their sense of self and belonging plays a major part in the child's development as they discover how to interact with others and appropriate behavioral responses. Trauma can also create an interference in the child's ability to make secure and safe attachments to others, opening the door to be exposed to other traumas and becoming a precursor to possible substance abuse.

Adolescence

The age range of 13–19 is a normal time for adolescents to be rebellious and push boundaries in efforts to define themselves and figure out who they really are outside of the family home. Boundaries within peer relationships are also pushed during this time, and a teenager's relationship with their friends starts to become more influential than the relationship with their parents. The notoriety that they gain from their friends can place a large amount of influence on their behavior and their willingness to experiment with drugs and alcohol in a social setting.

Take Matthew's Story

Fifteen-year-old Matthew has been recently placed into foster care after being in a violent physical altercation with his father. This isn't the first time that Matthew has experienced his father's tendency to be violent in the home and reported that he has been on the receiving end of the abuse since he was young. He reported that he has been drinking and smoking since the age of eight as a way to cope with the abuse. However, Matthew's anger about being removed from his family home has fueled his need to drink more and he has started to use drugs. He has become more rebellious in his foster home and at school and reported getting behind the wheel after drinking multiple times. His anger has led him to get into many physical fights with the neighborhood teens and has even woken up with a black eye after a night of drinking with no memory of how it happened.

Trauma and PTSD

At least two-thirds of adolescents have experienced or witnessed a traumatic event in their teenage years, putting this group at considerably high risk. Due to the perception that adolescents don't require as much supervision as younger children, they are more likely to be exposed to sexual violence and violence within the community, therefore creating a major health concern for this age group and a higher chance of developing the symptoms of psychological stressors. Being bullied at school can be the first stepping stone of traumatic stressors, and is a growing concern for children at this age. About 20% of high school students, grades 9 through 12, reported being the target of bullying in 2009 (Ouimette et al., 2014, pp. 95–114).

Dating and sexual relationships are a new experience for adolescents, but it is also a time of experiencing the world of sexual assault and dating violence for the first time. Data shows that the rate of dating violence experienced by teenage girls ranges from 20%–30%. Adolescent boys aren't always the culprit of dating violence, with 7% reporting being the victim of the assault. In 2020, it was reported that 12% of girls and almost 4% of boys, of high school age, had experienced some form of sexual violence by their partner (CDC, 2021).

Another big milestone emerges when a teen hits the age of 16, getting their driver's license. Teens see it as a rite of passage and another step toward their independence, but they are still considered to be high-risk drivers due to the difference in brain development compared to that of an adult driver. Since the part of their brain that weighs risks and consequences hasn't been fully formed yet, it isn't surprising that teen drivers have the highest rate of motor vehicle accidents. These accidents make adolescents more vulnerable to trauma if they are the cause or the passenger of a serious car crash.

The rate of reported PTSD cases among adolescents varies depending on the study. In 2003, a sample held nationwide over six months reported an estimated 5% for teens between the ages of 12–17. However, in 2007, a much lower percentage was reported in a sample of 14–16-year-olds, with 2.2% for possible PTSD and 0.4% with fully diagnosable PTSD (Ouimette et al., 2014, pp. 95–114).

PTSD and Substance Abuse

The initial usage of drugs and alcohol among adolescents has been linked to exposure to trauma, with the trauma preceding the initial use. However, it seems that the association between trauma and substance abuse is bidirectional. While the trauma may precede substance abuse in most cases, the use of drugs and alcohol makes the adolescent more susceptible to more trauma while they are under the influence. A delay in response and being prone to making risky decisions can put the teen in dangerous situations.

The comorbidity rate of adolescents with PTSD and Substance Abuse Disorder (SUD) is reported at approximately 11% in a community sample and around 47% in a clinical sample (Ouimette et al., 2014, pp. 95–114). The dual diagnosis of both of these disorders unsurprisingly has a larger impact on the functioning of adolescents than only being diagnosed with one of them.

Biological Considerations

The combination of PTSD and substance abuse can leave a lasting impact on an adolescent's brain development as they move into adulthood. Brain development occurs rapidly during adolescence, and chronic stress, especially traumatic stress, affects and disrupts the neurological functioning they need to mature. PTSD and SUD impair the development of the distal and proximal parts of the brain as the teen comes of age, creating significant cognitive impairments later on in life.

Chronic stress in one's life elevates the level of cortisol in the bloodstream. This elevated level can have multiple consequences for adolescents that are exposed to constant stressors, such as a decrease in hormones that are essential to puberty and a depletion of the brain's resources responsible for learning. Being exposed to trauma can decrease the volume in an adolescent's hippocampus, leading to impairments in their executive functioning, emotional control, and problems in their personal and social relationships. By adding heavy alcohol or narcotics use into the equation, the brain's cognitive functioning can be hindered further and have more lasting negative effects.

Behavioral and Psychosocial Considerations

Adolescence is marked by the shift away from their parents and moving closer to their peers, and being more prone to risk-taking behavior. The risks that they are willing to take bring with it the potential for physical and sexual violence, and becoming the underlying issue of subsequent substance abuse.

Establishing their individuality and an increasing need for privacy make a parent's ability to intervene in an adolescent's substance abuse a challenge. Teens find it extremely difficult to talk to parents and other adults about their distress, usually in fear of consequences for disclosing information about their sexual activities and risky behavior. Creating strong and established boundaries between what can be shared with parents and what should stay in the therapeutic setting can allow the adolescent to open up and resolve the stress caused by trauma.

Late Adolescence and Emerging Adulthood

The ages of 18–25 are considered to be the time where a person becomes an independent adult. It is a chance of discovery as they emerge from the stages of adolescence into adulthood. It is also a stage of finding freedom and having new responsibilities, along with discovering new risks and challenges as they navigate through life. Substance misuse and abuse, trauma, and PTSD fall into the category of these new risks.

Take Amy's Story

Nineteen-year-old Amy is a freshman in college. During her junior year in high school, she was sexually assaulted by a man that she assumed was a friend while attending a party. Following the assault, she has found herself to be extremely nervous and on edge while in large group settings. She does not go out of her way to avoid them though, acknowledging that socializing is an important part of life and the college experience. Amy focuses on her schoolwork during the week and does her best to abstain from drinking, but on the weekends, she drinks heavily with her friends to the point of blacking out. She finds that drinking in her dorm before a party allows her to become more comfortable in large groups. One Sunday morning, Amy wakes up on a dormitory floor with cuts and bruises all over her and no recollection of what happened the night before.

Trauma and PTSD

Out of any age group, young adults are the most vulnerable when it comes to exposure to traumatic experiences. Around two-thirds of young adults between the ages of 18–25 have experienced events that include dating violence, violent sexual assaults, and drunk driving. Among those young adults that reported their exposure, at least 9% of them show symptoms of post-traumatic stress disorder (Ouimette et al., 2014, pp. 95–114).

Biological Considerations

The reason for the vulnerability within this age group is how the brain processes the trauma. Underdeveloped brains have trouble focusing on how to move past the trauma, while the reward center of the brain has been developed for years. The reward circuitry leads to a greater need for exploration, risk-taking behaviors, and instant gratification. The combination of the underdeveloped brain and the fully developed reward center is linked to the vulnerability to trauma and the willingness to use substances to cope. The part of the brain that manages executive control and decision making, known as the prefrontal cortex, doesn't develop until later in adulthood. The differences in the timing of maturation of the parts in the brain make the years of late adolescence an inevitable risk.

Behavioral and Psychosocial Considerations

The gap between maturing internally and the external challenges of finding their independence and easy access to drugs and alcohol occur at the same time, making this time confusing and full of risks. Adulthood also brings on a new task of taking on new roles as far as social, educational, and workplace settings go. Trying to separate your work life from your social and family life is not an easy task as you learn who you are as an individual. These transitions in tasks can create a change in the use and amount of substances they use, and any involvement or problems with substances can compromise the ability to handle these transitions and roles.

Socializing with one's peers is especially important in young adulthood. Learning how to network socially and what is considered acceptable behavior in the social setting can determine how willing someone is to use drugs. If their peer group considers substance abuse a normal behavior, they will be more accustomed to taking part in substance abuse, and at times use them at extremely high levels.

Chapter 6:

Starting Your Recovery

When it comes to recovery, the use of imagery is much more than envisioning a story. It means using powerful images and making them mean something specific for you and your health while gaining control over your psyche. It means creating and making the most of your powerful image's message, while you set goals and find motivation in the recovery process.

Take Martha's Story

Martha grew up in a home where violence was rampant. Her dad regularly beat her mom, and there was nothing that she could do to stop it. As she moved into her teen years, she found herself in the same type of violent relationships. Now that she is older, she has become committed to finding a healthy partner and a relationship that makes her feel safe. She has come to realize that focusing on taking care of all of her partner's wants and needs, instead of her own, led to her being in her unhealthy past relationships. Martha would learn to shut down whenever there was a conflict or disagreement, just as she had when she was a child. She made the conscious choice to use an old-fashioned mercury thermometer as an image that pertains to her, measuring out and gauging how she feels when she is around certain people. She gauges how valued and appreciated she feels around some people, or how uncomfortable, mistreated, and controlled when she is around others. When someone gives her negative feelings, the temperature reading goes up and when she feels calm and relaxed, the temperature reading is extremely low. Martha even put a picture of a thermometer on the background of her phone as a helpful reminder. She is slowly becoming aware of what is going on around her and hopes that this newfound awareness leads her to a healthy relationship.

Images Can Improve Your Recovery

A visual image can be a powerful tool when it comes to healing and the recovery process. It can be used in all types of environments, from educational to medicinal use. The medical field uses images during childbirth, or when helping with chronic pain, and cancer treatments. Research has shown that people heal faster and feel a decrease in their pain when they use healing and calming images. It has also shown that the use of positive imagery lowers one's stress levels, improves digestion, and lowers heart rate while negative imagery has an adverse effect. Imagery can also help performance levels among professional athletes, doctors, and musicians. Imagining each step of the game, surgery, or note strengthens their ability to perform their jobs.

The Image Gives You Purpose and Motivation

Finding an image that works for you is half the battle. Try picturing an image that motivates you and gives you purpose, and see how that image makes you feel. Does it make you feel protected, empowered, and connected to the world around you? Does it reinforce your power over your trauma and symbolize your recovery from your addiction? Your image can be of your choosing, whether it is a physical object, a photograph, or a drawing, as long as it means something to you. Here are some examples that may be helpful for you.

- Judy chose a picture of her daughter as a baby for inspiration. The photo pushes her to keep going and seek treatment, even when she is reluctant.

- Margo chose a hot air balloon floating through the sky as a reminder that she doesn't have to remain stagnant in her recovery. She can sail through her recovery, remember to get up and get moving and take care of herself.

- Dave chose the logo of the school that he hopes to get into one day as a way to keep him grounded in reality and remind himself that he still has a chance in this world.

In each example, you will notice that there are three parts to each image they chose: a specific image, a personal meaning to the image that promotes their recovery, and actions that are specific to their personal recovery process. Judy chose treatment, Margo chose to take care of herself, and Dave chose a specific school that he is working to get into.

Explore . . . Create Your Healing Image

There are four questions to ask yourself when choosing your healing image:

- What image will work for your recovery?

- What is the meaning of this image for you?

- What are the actions that this image is attached to in your recovery process?

- How will you keep this image present in your everyday life?

For example, if you were to choose an Olympic swimmer as your image, the meaning may be that you are an athlete in recovery. Swimmers need to keep practicing and keep their minds sharp in order to win. The actions attached to this image would be to keep working on your recovery every day, even if you don't feel like it. There are days that swimmers don't want to practice, but they do it anyway. You will choose to abstain from using drugs and alcohol, go to all doctor's appointments, and get a restful sleep every night. Just like a focused swimmer, you will cut ties with anyone or anything that poses as a distraction from your goals. In order to keep this image present in your everyday life, you may upload it on the background of your phone, or print off a picture of a swimmer on a podium and put it in your wallet or anywhere that you will see it throughout the day.

Carry It With You

Finding ways to make that image present in your everyday life will also keep the image alive in your heart and at the forefront of your mind. It will be there for you when you are struggling and become your personal piece of paradise. That image will become your sense of calmness when you are in distress. You can create reminders of the image by putting it everywhere you look throughout the day such as in the examples below.

- Place the image as the background on all of your electrical devices (laptop, cellphone, tablet, desktop screen).

- Place the image in frequented rooms around your home and your workplace (bedside table, refrigerator, bathroom mirror, desk drawer).

- Put it on or in an object that you can carry with you (wallet, keychain, necklace charm).

Chapter 7:

Create Your Own Recovery Plan

Creating a plan personally catered to your needs increases your chances for a successful recovery. Acknowledging your weaknesses or downfalls is a major step when making a plan that will help reduce your harmful behaviors and replace them with positive or safe behaviors. Your plan can easily be integrated into any treatment approach you choose and offers you other strategies you can use in efforts to maintain your success during and after treatment.

Take David's Story

David considers his new healthier behavior to be a measurement of how well he is doing. However, sometimes his thoughts are like a foggy field and he is unable to see where he is going in life or the potential risks and dangerous situations directly in front of him. Using his actions as a map to lead him through the fog, marking them as positive or negative, he can keep track of where he is going and how he is doing in the recovery process. He realized that sometimes he can't trust his thoughts, as the life of addiction and PTSD told him nothing but lies. David learned how to keep track of certain behaviors, what he is doing, how often, and what triggered him to do them so that he can tip the scales in his favor. Keeping track of his actions has helped him immensely because the tracking is for him to know only. Not for therapy, just for him. Some days it is a struggle not to judge himself and not pressure himself to try to change everything at once, but he manages to take it day by day. After accomplishing one goal he had to make a mental note before choosing another one, knowing what needs to be changed, why, and what the first steps are. His personal recovery plan allows him to know exactly where he is, not where he thinks he is or should be.

What Are You Looking for in Recovery?

The main goal in recovery is to increase your positive behaviors and decrease your negative behaviors. Decreasing negative behaviors in your addiction may include not: drinking excessively, gambling, overspending, overconsuming food, exercising past your physical limit, and using illicit drugs. Decreasing behaviors in your trauma may include not: isolating yourself, self-harming, and hurting others maliciously. Or your recovery may look like a mixture of decreasing both categories of behavior.

The goal for a successful recovery plan is finding a way to tip the scale in your favor, as David did, and making sure the weight of your positive behaviors is more than the weight of the negatives. By adding the positives and subtracting the negatives on your recovery scale, you will find it easier to manage the belief that you can live without behaviors that are considered unsafe for you. Some people have trouble avoiding unsafe and risky behaviors, as it is the only way they know how to live and without it, their life seems empty. The idea that living without risk seems intolerable, but it's a process of growth and building yourself up to see that life outside of addiction and trauma can be much more optimistic than they ever thought.

Explore . . . Create Your "Tip the Scales" Recovery Plan

Creating your own "tip the scales" recovery plan is a simple series of questions. Don't overwhelm yourself and try to rush through them, just answer them one by one.

1. **What negative or unsafe behavior do you want to increase?**

For example, do you want to stop drinking excessively? Or, not yelling so much at your spouse and kids? Do you want to stop eating too much or watching porn? Do you want to stop isolating yourself or self-harming?

Once you choose a behavior, focus on it specifically. Make sure that this specific behavior is currently wreaking havoc on your life and that of your family—not one that you have already worked on.

2. **How much or how often are you doing this unsafe/negative behavior?**

For example, are you drinking one to two bottles of wine a week? Are you staying up every night watching porn or television? Do you spend more than your weekly paycheck in a night? Are you having arguments or screaming at your family members at least two to three times a week? Are you taking or misusing substances daily?

Your answer will be specific to the behavior that you chose. Remember to be specific about numbers as in times per week, amount of money spent, or glasses drank. It is okay if it varies from week to week, or even day to day, just focus on your normal amount. Be honest with yourself about how often you do these behaviors, as some people are surprised at the amount they partake in their unsafe behavior once they actually focus on it. Knowing and acknowledging the truth is the first step in realizing that you can work on your behavior.

3. **What is the main goal in decreasing this behavior?**

For example, "I want to cut down watching television to one show or movie a day."

"I want to cut down on self-harming until I can stop completely."

"I want to decrease my drinking to one glass of wine a week."

Next, you will want to choose a positive behavior to replace the negative one. Substitution is needed if you want to make a lasting change in your life. Choosing a positive or safe behavior and focusing on it, can help rewire the brain into a positive mindset, making the sensation to enact the negative behaviors weaker. People with severe unsafe behaviors have been able to be successful in their recovery plan. So just remember that even if it seems like it may not be working for you, just keep at it.

1. **What positive or safe behavior would you like to increase?**

For example: bake more often, spend more time with family, try out new clothing or hairstyle, go bowling, clean your house or bedroom, answer emails, do something creative, call a hotline if needed, organize your day with a schedule, go outside, walk through nature.

Staying active helps keep your mind busy, not only building up your resistance to the negative behaviors but distracting you from the cravings as well.

2. **How often do you currently work on your safe behaviors? How often would you like to work on them?**

Think about how often you work on your safe behavior per week, then increase it at an appropriate and realistic amount. It seems simple, but the amount that you devote to your safe and positive behaviors is powerful for your recovery. Think of it as changing the channel on the television, soaking up the information on a new show can quiet down the chatter and divert you from thinking about the unsafe behavior.

The last portion of creating your own recovery plan is tracking your progress. Keep track of how well you are doing regarding decreasing your negative behaviors and increasing your positive behaviors while tracking how often you are craving the negative. Start small and try it for a week to see how it feels for you. Don't make it your whole life, just make a small effort in the task. Think of tracking as gaining valuable feedback. If you notice the negative or unsafe behaviors are getting out of hand, you are more aware of the issue and can figure out how to deal with the problem and get in front of it. Some people find electronic trackers on their phones, a printed calendar, or timers to be helpful tools to track how often and for how long the duration of the behavior occurs.

Success Strategies

You can give your recovery plan an extra boost with a few methods, further tipping your scale in the direction of your success. Using at least five of these methods will give you that extra boost in motivation toward a healthy and happy recovery.

- *Figure out your why, leading your way to the how.* Maybe your addiction has caused you to lose custody of your children. Your reason for recovery may be so that you can get your children back, and your children will get their parent back.

- *Make your recovery plan fun.* Working toward recovery doesn't have to be boring. You could write all of your safe behaviors down on a list, close your eyes and pick one. You could draw popsicle sticks with a positive behavior written on them. Make your safe and healthier life enjoyable.

- *Don't get stuck thinking that recovery is all-or-nothing.* A small slip doesn't mean that you have failed, things happen and so does life. Just chalk it up as a loss, and put yourself back on the right path.

- *Share your plan with close family and friends that want to see you succeed.* Finding positive and influential people in your life to share your plan with can help you when you are struggling to stay on the right path and backslide a little bit. They can also keep you accountable. Just remember that there will be some people that may feel threatened or angry that you are moving forward with your life, do your best to avoid them.

- *Stick with your safe behavior for at least a half-hour.* Thirty minutes of busy work is the amount of time that it takes to reduce most cravings or urges for unsafe behaviors. If the craving or urge doesn't pass after a half-hour, add another one until the feeling subsides.

- *Recovery means creating progress, not perfection.* Sometimes a small slip makes people dealing with addiction and trauma-related problems blame themselves and feel at fault, creating a self-loathing spiral of destruction. Don't beat yourself up if things don't work out how you planned, just get back up, dust yourself off, and try again.

- *Be prepared for what you should expect.* In the early stages of recovery, be prepared to go through inner conflicts with your urges and cravings. It will be as if a little angel on your shoulder is fighting with the devil on the other. You will find yourself easily triggered by reminders of your past unsafe behaviors. A particular time of night may be a reminder of opening a bottle of wine. Remind yourself that sticking with your plan and abstaining from the behavior will become easier over time, and eventually, the cravings will subside.

- *Remove all temptations.* There will always be temptations in the world, waiting to trigger you when you least expect it. However, you have control over your physical environment. You can remove any temptations that are in your home, throw them away if you feel triggered, or give them away to someone where it is unavailable to you. Walk a different way to work if passing by a liquor store triggers a craving for a bottle of liquor. Taking control over your environment and your triggers also means taking a part of your life back.

- *Give your plan 30 days.* Remember that it takes about a month to create a new habit. Stick it out and see what progress you make.

- *Don't wait until tomorrow. Do it today.* All lifestyle changes create the temptation of waiting until a specific time to start. Think about the people that want to diet, it's always "I'll start next week or Monday, or after the holidays." Why put your health and future in jeopardy with something that you could start today, right this very second, and work toward a full recovery?

- *Reward yourself for sticking to the plan.* Sticking with a plan for a week or a month is no easy feat. Rewarding yourself with a healthy reward gives you something to be proud of. It may help to schedule something in advance. For example: if I stick with my plan for a whole month, I will reward myself with that cute pair of shoes I want at the mall.

Consider Entering a Treatment Program

If you are having a hard time restricting and reducing your unsafe and negative behaviors, don't be afraid to consider entering a treatment program. You don't have to go through the recovery process alone, especially when there are so many resources available to help you in this journey. Getting over trauma or addiction is almost impossible for anyone to do on their own. When combined they will surely need professional help. Adding treatment to your recovery plan can help you get on track and maintain any effort you will be making to start and stay in the recovery process, and most importantly to maintain it afterward. For further information on integrative treatment approaches and choosing which one may be the best for you, you can refer to chapters 9–12.

Chapter 8:

Find a Treatment Focusing on

Addiction and Trauma

Finding the appropriate treatment to deal with your addiction and trauma can seem like you are going down the rabbit hole. Some treatments are problem-specific, only dealing with one problem at a time and putting the others on the back burner. However, finding a treatment that focuses on trauma and addiction at the same time can open up your mind, and your heart, so that you can get the help you truly need.

Take Lily's Story

Lily is a child abuse survivor, which led to a serious drug addiction that lasted until her 30s. She spent most of this time avoiding the thought of what happened to her, leaving her childhood memories a blur. She used drugs as a way to forget, giving her a reason to live. Through treatment, Lily learned that when she is craving drugs, that there is a reminder of her past trauma that she needs to deal with in order to take care of herself. However, this skill didn't come to her immediately, because she was unable to see how her addiction was associated with her trauma. She came to realize that the violence that she witnessed and endured in her childhood was inescapable, but when she was using, she felt like she was finally alive. When entering a treatment center for the first time, Lily was told that they would focus on her addiction first and her trauma later, but that day never came. Years later, she finally found a counselor that helped her work on both issues and their recovery, giving her different ideas to try that may help her.

Many people, like Lily, don't realize how strong the link between trauma and addiction actually is. They also don't realize that the link is especially important in the recovery process. In order to recover from one, you have to use the same skills to recover from the other. Research shows that, if given the choice, more people prefer to work on both issues at the same time, rather than one at a time, stating that it makes the recovery process more powerful (Najavits, 2019b, pp. 1–8).

What People Start Saying to Themselves When in Recovery

The way that you think when first starting the recovery process changes over time. Unloading the thoughts of trauma and removing the substances from the cloudy brain can clear your head, allowing you to think rationally and more positively. Before treatment starts, one may automatically assume that it won't work and relapse is inevitable. However, after some time, the thoughts of "my memories haunt me" change into "I am no longer afraid of my memories." "Using drugs makes it possible for me to be sexual" turns into "I no longer have to use drugs to have sex." "Drinking alcohol keeps me from killing myself" slowly turns into "I am capable of taking care of my mental health without using substances." "I hate everything about myself" finally turns into "I know who I am now, and I know my worth."

Why Is the Traditional Approach Not the Best for You?

In an addiction treatment setting, the treatment of one's psychological trauma has always been put on hold, or on a "wait until later" status. Teaching how to abstain from substance abuse, working on damaged relationships, and issues in the workplace, but leaving out the recovery process for the underlying cause of the addiction. In the trauma-related treatment setting, only the event(s) that the person went through are focused on with the belief that once the trauma is dealt with, the addiction will simply go away. There is also the belief that their unsafe and addictive behaviors are only used as an attempt to avoid the trauma. The differences in both treatments would lead someone to be in multiple programs to deal with different issues for their dual diagnoses. Sometimes, the traditional approach isn't best for dealing with a substance abuse addiction with an underlying history of trauma because most treatments are considered to be "problem-specific" (Carruth, 2006) and the therapist's knowledge and understanding of both disorders are limited.

Take the Approach That Works on Trauma and Addiction Together

It is a true 'aha' moment when you discover how strongly your trauma and addiction are linked while you are in recovery. Using a new approach that focuses on both trauma *and* your addiction where your therapist or counselor is informed on both treatments can open new doors for you, allowing you to become more motivated and feel more understood in your recovery. Having trauma and addiction-informed help gives an extra boost in getting one to realize that if you have both disorders, you can get help with both without having to be enrolled in multiple programs that only focus on one specific issue. The new approach comes with the understanding that while working on trauma or addiction recovery, the symptoms or cravings of the other may flare up; therefore, needing more attention. It allows you to work on both disorders at the same time so that you can embrace all of the help that you can, laying the foundation that there are many ways to heal and it's how you work on these problems that matter. There are many reasons behind addictive and trauma-related behavior, and learning how your genes, culture, environment, and gender play a role in these behaviors can be integrated into your treatment.

Best Self in Recovery

Different situations bring out different versions of all of us, whether it's the best version or the worst. Knowing and accepting that version is a good sign because you will soon discover that just because you are the worst version of yourself right now, that it can all change once you change your situation. It is possible to find the best version of yourself again, you just have to keep at it. You may have lost yourself along the way due to the trauma you endured and the addiction leading you astray from everything you knew about yourself. At one point, you may have looked in the mirror and had no idea who that person was looking back at you.

Discovering one's best self while in recovery is different for everyone. Some people want to become someone who is seen as more responsible and can be trusted. Some people want to become loving parents again and have healthy relationships with other people. Others want to be able to have impulses or cravings without the need to act on them, but rather become assertive and be able to tell others their wants and needs. So, what do you want? What version of yourself do you want to become?

Think about those questions for a moment, and think about all the possible selves you could become.

- Do you want to become an *emotional* self, and learn how to deal with and respond to your feelings appropriately?

- Do you want to become a *relationship* self, and learn how to respond to other people and their needs?

- Do you want to become a *work/school* self, and discover how to achieve your goals without letting your trauma and addiction get in the way?

- Do you want to become a *spiritual* self, and learn how you can relate to a higher power and surround yourself with others that do the same?

- Do you want to become a *physical* self, and take better care of yourself through diet and exercise?

- Do you want to become a *recovery* self, and take your trauma and addiction seriously and put it all behind you once and for all?

Chapter 9:

Choosing the Right Therapy for You: CBT

For any treatment to succeed, you, the patient, should be receptive, and it should be compatible with who you are. The main purpose of the next few chapters on treatment is to give you a peek into what to expect if you chose one treatment over the other, which will save you time and money, and offer you a better chance of success. Cognitive Behavioral Therapy (CBT) is one of the most recommended approaches when it comes to the treatment of PTSD and addiction.

Take Jasmin's Story

Jasmine was first diagnosed with PTSD when she was in treatment for her cocaine addiction, much to her own surprise. Her counselor finally figured it out after a deep conversation surrounding the abuse she suffered as a child; pointing it out to Jasmin that she had a PTSD problem, not just a problem with cocaine. Jasmin was in disbelief, not believing that it was possible to have both conditions at the same time. Her denial was short-lived and she was relieved that there was a name for what was wrong with her—and there was a cure. Now that she was aware of both conditions, she could take care of them the right way. With the help of her counselor, she could dig down and find where the underlying problem came from, then work on it. She started to see herself differently, she no longer saw herself as an outsider or a freak. Rather, she started to see herself as human, a hopeful human with a few problems to work on.

The Five Stages of PTSD

To understand how treatment for PTSD works, you first have to acknowledge and understand the five stages of post-traumatic stress disorder that people go through when they are attempting to recover from the exposure of trauma.

Stage One: The Emergency Stage. The first stage is also known as the "outcry" stage. During this time, you will feel an intense response to everything around you and your anxiety will be at an extremely high level. It is normally the beginning of the natural "fight or flight" instinct kicking in.

Stage Two: The Numbing Stage. The second stage is also known as the "denial" stage. PTSD comes with a concerning amount of denial, often regarding the emotions that you are struggling with stemming from the traumatic event. Numbing and avoidance make dealing with what happened to you much easier, even though the symptoms of denial are increasing your stress and anxiety level.

Stage Three: The Intrusive-Repetitive Stage. Despite the person's best efforts to avoid and deny their emotions, those feelings have interjected themselves into their subconscious, creating recurrent nightmares and flashbacks. During this stage, you may feel extremely anxious and on the edge of your seat. The third stage is considered to be the most destructive stage of the stages, but it is also the best time for you to confront the trauma causing your PTSD so you can regain control over your life.

Stage Four: The Transition Stage. During the fourth stage, you can officially start to move toward recovery. By transitioning into a higher level of acceptance you will be able to understand what happened to you and the impact that the event had on your life so that you can finally start to heal.

Stage Five: The Integration Stage. The fifth, and final, stage happens when you start to work on your PTSD recovery plan. You learn how to use healthy coping skills in everyday situations so that you can address and reduce your PTSD symptoms. This is also a time for extreme patience because it does take some time to get to the point where you no longer struggle without regressing to a previous stage.

Prolonged Exposure Therapy for PTSD

Prolonged exposure therapy is a specific subtype of cognitive behavioral therapy that helps someone that has been exposed to trauma gradually confront their fears, memories, and feelings as they relate to the traumatic event. Exposure to trauma, especially chronic trauma, makes most people do whatever they can to avoid what happened, only deepening their fears. Prolonged exposure, or PE, requires them to face the trauma that they have been avoiding, which in turn decreases the symptoms and severity of their PTSD and shows them that they are no longer in danger or need to avoid the memories. This therapeutic treatment usually takes place twice a week for about nine to twelve weeks, each appointment lasting between an hour to an hour and a half.

There are two types of exposure used during this therapy, imaginal and in vivo. Imaginal exposure is used during the therapy session and requires the patient to describe every detail of the traumatic event in the present tense as they are guided by the therapist. When the patient is done going over the details, they will work closely with their therapist to dissect and process the emotions they felt as they went through the exposure. The session is usually recorded for the patient to listen to in the safety of their home between sessions so that they can process their emotions even further and practice some calming breathing exercises.

In vivo exposure is assigned as the patient's homework between the sessions, where they confront the stimuli that they have been avoiding. The therapist will work with the patient to come up with a list of stimuli that triggers memories of the trauma, like specific places, objects, or people. They will then come up with a plan to put the in vivo exposure in place and how to go about the exposure to the stimuli. The patient is encouraged to make it a challenge as they gradually expose themselves to the stimuli and confront the fear that they have held onto for so long. In doing so they will feel a sense of success as they cope with the emotions associated with the trauma.

Exposure-Based Treatment and Early Childhood Trauma

Treatment based solely on exposure has had mixed reviews when it comes to the subject of early childhood trauma, especially sexual abuse. The main concern being that the exposure targets the fear and anxiety relating to the abuse are unable to be diminished, and the patient's belief that the abuse is their fault isn't accurately addressed. These guilty beliefs are usually to blame for the ongoing PTSD symptoms and aren't specifically and directly addressed during the exposure process, as it only addresses the fears and anxiety due to the trauma. However, other research has found that frequent exposure shows changes to cognitive reasoning, including the belief of fault, do happen when the abuse is revisited through imaginal exposure. One study found that the process of CBT or exposure therapy alone didn't work as well as using both types of therapy together; and concluding that if severe childhood trauma is presented within the patients PTSD symptoms, that exposure therapy would be greatly beneficial to their progress. Within a sample of patients that were found to be alcohol-dependent and successfully treated for their PTSD symptoms with Prolonged Exposure therapy, 84% of them reported being either sexually or physically abused before the age of 13 (Ouimette et al., 2014, pp. 253–279). Even though trauma and the associated memories that stem from childhood abuse may complicate the treatment of an adult, it in no way makes exposure therapy less effective.

CBT New Findings Still Linger Toward the Separation of Treatments

While many physicians and therapists recommend the dual treatment for trauma and addiction, some are concerned that bringing up triggering trauma while in treatment for addiction may cause a relapse or impede the patient's progress. However, whether the treatment is trauma-based or using the relapse prevention approach, CBT therapists help their patients break the link between unhealthy choices, unsafe behaviors, negative feelings, and learn how to react differently in the future without the use of unhealthy or risky coping mechanisms.

Acceptance and Commitment Therapy (ACT)

Acceptance and Commitment Therapy, or ACT, shares the same concepts as exposure therapy, in the way of teaching the patient how to process the trauma that they have been avoiding. It identifies that avoidance of the symptoms of trauma and PTSD establish and maintain the reasoning behind their unhealthy coping mechanisms, with substance abuse being the most relative example. Along with substance abuse, is the use of self-harm, self-isolation, and the display of dissociative symptoms. ACT is different from other CBT methods, with the therapist using the alternative of avoidance and using an acceptance approach. However, it does share the same cognitive processes as CBT using the premise of automatic thoughts and changing the patient's intermediate and core beliefs in order to alleviate their symptoms. ACT works on helping the patient function in the real world despite their symptoms. It also works on the reduction of impact on their behavioral, emotional, cognitive processing. The specific techniques that ACT uses work for both substance abuse and PTSD symptoms by creating room for acceptance and change.

Chapter 10:

Choosing the Right Therapy for You: Psychodynamic Psychotherapy

Psychodynamic therapy is used and found to be effective for the vast majority of mental illnesses, including anxiety, stress, depression, and panic with their related physical ailments. This type of therapy focuses on the roots of the patient's emotional and psychological suffering using various methods of self-examination and self-reflection. The close relationship between the therapist and patient works as a window to look into what patterns are causing the most problems in the patient's life in order to alleviate their symptoms and help them lead a happier and healthier life.

Take Brad's Story

Brad did his civic duty and served three tours in Iraq. However, when he returned home, he found himself full of rage. His anger worked for him while he was in combat, but when he came back, it took a toll on his everyday life. His friends stopped hanging out with him, and his wife and children were terrified of him. Brad's military instincts were slowly breaking up his family. He started to live in fear that he would turn into his father, a rage-aholic after he returned from World War II. He started to see that his rage was part of his PTSD, and he refused to let it take over his life. Brad's rage had become an addiction, and the only way to fix that addiction was to accept his flaws and own his actions. Today, Brad tries his best to take responsibility for his feelings, instead of putting the rage onto anyone around him. He still gets triggered from time to time, but he has learned to relax when he is stressed and to walk away rather than blow up.

What to Expect in Psychodynamic Psychotherapy

There are several components to psychodynamic psychotherapy sessions, including exploring the resistance of the patient's emotions, focusing on the effect and expression of their emotions, identifying their patterns of feelings, thoughts, relationships, and experiences. Psychodynamic psychotherapy also emphasizes the patient's past, while showing how it relates to their present problems. It focuses on their personal experiences while creating an empathetic relationship with their therapist in order to explore the patient's personality, mind, and psyche.

When a patient has a comorbid substance abuse disorder or addiction and a history of trauma, the therapist helps the patient understand how their substance abuse started and why it was sustained, along with the impact, meaning, and context of their trauma and symptoms. The patient's acknowledgment of the trauma and its impact on their life guides the aspects of all of their personal relationships, especially their therapeutic relationship so that they can focus on relapse prevention. The work needed for relapse prevention is similar to traditional trauma and addiction treatment, such as the 12-step recovery program.

Feel Your Feelings and Express Them Appropriately

Psychodynamic psychotherapists give their patients an immense amount of support as they help them identify their feelings and how to express them appropriately. It is a common understanding that one of the major reasons for an addiction relapse is because the patient has a lot of powerful emotions that they are unable to express or deal with appropriately without the help of unsafe coping mechanisms. The relapse for trauma-related problems or PTSD symptoms have a similar reason; however, the reason for their relapse is usually self-loathing and believing that their feelings aren't valid or they are wrong about the abuse. Both disorders find the emotions to be overwhelming, and it is understandable how they feel that they cannot handle them on their own.

One of the main purposes of psychodynamic psychotherapy is to teach these people how to gradually allow themselves to feel, express, and embrace these emotions. The ability to take these steps is significant in the recovery process. People that have been victimized have spent their entire lives being told that their feelings about the abuse, and their feelings in general, are wrong, so they are extremely sensitive to how their therapist will respond to their varying emotional states. The therapist will create a safe space for these patients, teaching them how to accept their emotions, avoid being overwhelmed, and reminding them that they will be able to get through their hard times.

Identify and Stop Unproductive Patterns

These specialized therapists will work with their patients to identify and discover patterns that are considered unproductive to their livelihood. The patterns that consist of their feelings, behaviors, thoughts, and relationships are focused on so that they can interrupt them if they are harmful to their emotional, behavioral, and mental health. Psychodynamic psychotherapists specifically focus on what and if their patterns are made consciously or subconsciously, while CBT therapists specifically focus on thinking and behaviors. Since psychodynamic psychotherapy uses the same principle beliefs as other types of treatments, including addiction treatment, many of their methods cannot be used if the patient is currently using substances.

Stages of Integrated Recovery

Psychodynamic psychotherapy's use of focusing on the past is extremely effective in helping patients with a history of trauma. The point of focusing on the patient's traumatic past is so that they can learn from it, allow themselves to grieve, and learn that they do not have to repeat the cycle. Three specific stages allow the patient to accomplish this goal.

Stage One

The first stage of integrated recovery in trauma and addiction treatment is to establish a feeling of personal safety. When it comes to substance abuse, safety can only be found by abstaining from drugs and alcohol. During trauma-related treatment, the priority is to establish a feeling of being physically safe. Early on in treatment, all of the patients need to be trained in skills that will help them deal with cravings and urges to use and abuse substances, learn how to set limits with other people, how to plan for emergencies or scary situations, and relapses in their substance use.

For patients that don't seek treatment until years after the abuse or trauma happened, the therapist has to create a feeling of psychological safety, rather than physical, so that they can lay the foundation to recover and heal. Creating a feeling of psychological safety can be difficult to establish, but once it is accomplished, the patient can finally feel safe with their feelings and emotions. The patient will be able to learn how and when they need to ask for help, how to manage their flashbacks and nightmares, and feel safe in a therapeutic setting. Feeling safe with a therapist is important because, in the case of a patient that is unaware of their past trauma, they may not know why they can't trust their therapist. They may be worried that, like everyone else in their past, that therapist or counselor may use the information that they share with them against them. Therapists combat this distrust by creating an alliance with their patients, by being honest with them, showing authenticity, talking with clarity, and being concise.

Stage Two

The second stage of integrated therapy focuses on helping the patient learn about themselves and remember who they were before their trauma and addiction. This is accomplished by the patient retelling their therapist the story of their life, so they can put the pieces of their past back together like a puzzle. Piecing their past together helps the patient to understand the relationship between their trauma and their addiction. This understanding is pertinent in helping the patient create their personal relapse prevention and recovery plan. Their personal recovery plan helps the patient identify risk situations, and ways to manage their emotions, cravings, and urges to use substances by using healthy coping skills instead. Retelling their past and dissecting it helps the patient let go of the belief that they are responsible for what happened to them and only responsible for how they take care of themselves and their recovery.

The second phase helps the patient to assign responsibilities where they belong for what happened, their feelings, and their attitude about their past trauma. Placing responsibility where it belongs and redefining their history, gives the patient a new perspective on their past and their current life. After redefining their history, the patient may start to feel like they are no longer stuck or hopeless any longer, that they are no longer a victim, and have an improved self-image.

This phase also allows the patient to grieve and mourn their past. Sigmund Freud has established the link between the ability to grieve loss and trauma, depression, and disappointments with the ability to accept the circumstance and feel motivated to keep going (Freud & Phillips, 2005). In treatment, grieving is an important component of preventing relapse in substance abuse and PTSD symptoms.

In psychodynamic psychotherapy, the therapist has to be prepared for heightened emotions during this stage, and the possible transference of those emotions onto them. Their patients may feel love, hate, anger, disappointment, rage, or sadness and direct them toward their therapist. It is normal for the patient to feel like the recovery and therapeutic process is taking too long during this time.

Stage Three

The third, and final, stage of the integrated recovery process is focused on maintaining sobriety and using new coping skills, along with reconnecting to the outside world and learning how to be supportive of others. For people that have been victimized and know who the perpetrator is, the therapist may advise the patient to confront the person during this stage. Confronting those that harmed them may help the patient validate their feelings about their circumstances. However, for some patients, a confrontation may not be the way to go for them for safety reasons. In that case, the therapist will arrange a psychological confrontation, where the patient can write a letter detailing what they would say to their perpetrator and read it out loud, in a safe therapeutic setting. This works in the process of accepting what happened to them and releasing their bottled emotions.

The third stage of recovery is also a time where people start to feel like themselves again, often referred to as 'reconnection' by therapists. It is considered reconnecting because the patient starts to feel connected to themselves and other people more healthily and productively. They continue the productive work by establishing new goals to create the life that they have dreamed of for themselves. For many trauma survivors, this is also the best time to try to reconnect with their families, but only with the exception that the family will be able to respond correctly to the patient's progress and be supportive of their journey.

Since this is the last stage in the integrated recovery process, it is a time when the patient gradually mentally and physically begins to separate themselves from the therapeutic setting. The gradual termination of their therapy services allows the patient to transfer their reliance and support from their therapist to their friends and family, working to resolve any and all transference that occurred during the second stage.

Chapter 11:

Choosing the Right Therapy for You: 12-Steps Program

The 12-steps recovery program is one of the most famous and the most attended drug addiction program. The guided program was initially created by the founders of Alcoholics Anonymous to help people suffering from substance abuse overcome their addiction. The program has maintained its success by allowing its members to adapt the steps to fit their needs.

Take Karla's Story

Karla has been in therapy since she was a teenager due to multiple sexual assaults and an addiction to food and alcohol. She can definitively say that in those years she has seen the best and the worst counselors in the field. One counselor even became angry with Karla at one point when she was having suicidal thoughts. He would ask her why she wasn't just using the coping skills that he had taught her. The counselor couldn't seem to grasp the concept that when she is thinking irrationally, it becomes impossible for her to use the coping skills. Her favorite counselor was amazing, and she saw her for years. The counselor taught Karla how to see the good parts of herself when she couldn't bear to look at herself in the mirror. She started to finally see her worth, and that her life was worth living. The counselor was patient with her when she experienced flashbacks about her childhood sexual abuse, and helped her break them down without pushing her too hard. The counselor also taught her how to use practical skills to handle her day-to-day life, and hung in there when Karla relapsed where other counselors would tell her that she wasn't motivated enough to stay clean. She came to realize that a good counselor shows empathy toward their patients and accepts what they say as the truth. The bad ones just judge their patient's experiences rather than trying to understand what they are trying to say.

What Is a 12-Step Program?

A 12-step program is a group that focuses on chemical dependency with the concept of like-minded people helping each other get and stay sober. Sharing the same principle beliefs as Alcoholics Anonymous (AA), there are now 12-step programs and groups available for a large range of addictions, such as substance abuse and gambling. The program is more effective for people that are chemically dependent than those that have a history of trauma. However, there are concerns about how appropriate the program is for people that are chemically dependent and have been exposed to trauma.

Expected Outcomes of the 12 Steps

The 12 steps each have their own role in the recovery process. The model provides the person in recovery with encouragement, support, and the ability to take accountability for everything they have done while under the influence. How each individual interprets the steps vary, and it is up to them how they implement the steps based on their belief system. The step model goes as follows:

Step 1: Being honest with themselves. This includes admitting that they have a problem with alcohol, or their unhealthy addiction, and the role that their behavior plays in their life.

Step 2: Changing their attitude. The person has to be willing to believe in a 'Higher Power,' someone who guides them and gives them hope.

Step 3: Finding a sense of faith. The person discovers their reliance on and a belief in a 'Higher Power' for guidance and strength.

Step 4: Looking inward and self-reflection. The person will start to understand their strengths and weaknesses and how their character defects affect their actions and thoughts.

Step 5: Learning to be humble. The person has to admit their mistakes and be willing to accept their character defects so they can improve their life.

Step 6: Become willing. The person has to be ready to ask their 'Higher Power' to remove their weaknesses and shortcomings in order to improve their life.

Step 7: Practice humility. The person is ready to ask their 'Higher Power' to help them remove any obstacles that are in their way of self-improvement.

Step 8: Be understanding. The person has to make a list of the people that they have harmed while they were in their addiction and be willing to ask for their forgiveness.

Step 9: Time for atonement. The person asks the people that they harmed for forgiveness.

Step 10: Gaining a sense of insightfulness. The person is required to reflect on their character defects on a daily basis.

Step 11: Strengthening one's faith. The person has to be willing to improve their relationship with their 'Higher Power' and ask for their guidance.

Step 12: Being of service to others. The person is now able to help other people and use the program in all aspects of their life.

Trauma and 12-Step Program

12-step programs may not be best for people suffering from trauma, especially childhood trauma. If the person can abstain from using drugs and alcohol, the intrusive thoughts and symptoms from their trauma may present themselves. If one chooses to follow them, they need to be completed with professional assistance to work on the trauma. With the help of a therapist, someone with both disorders can start to understand the relationship between their substance abuse and their trauma-related symptoms. Both disorders have their own specific and unique needs in order to be successful in their treatment, and if those needs are unmet, the person seeking treatment is at a disadvantage and likely to develop more problems. Paige Ouimette stated in a 1998 study that, when asking a sample of people that had co-occurring PTSD and substance abuse disorders, it was found that 40% of them shared a specific fear of talking about their trauma and other people finding out. This fear acted as a barrier to seek help. Another barrier that was discovered in the study was the fact that people with dual diagnoses were often misdiagnosed as having only one of the disorders, further delaying the need to receive the help they needed (Ouimette et al., 1998).

Chapter 12:

Choosing the Right Therapy for You: Integrating Creative Arts

A 2016 study held by Drexel University found that integrated creative arts, also known as art therapy, helps patients reduce their cortisol levels caused by high levels of stress by a significant amount (Kaimal et al., 2016). Creating art helps the patient resolve their issues surrounding their trauma, while subsequently identifying and exploring the roots of their substance abuse and addiction.

Take Simone's Story

Simone is in the beginning stages of her recovery from alcohol use and past trauma. Before she started treatment, she found it extremely difficult to think positively about herself. She realized that getting out of that negative frame of mind was possible as she watched other people do it and become successful in their recovery. Now when she finds herself in a difficult and dark place in her life, she needs to keep walking toward the light. Walking toward the light was just a baby step in this journey, then people started to show up to help her. Once she received help, she felt like she may actually be able to make it through the process.

How Can Art or Creative Therapies Help You?

Adding creative arts into your addiction and trauma therapy provides a lot of benefits. People that took different types of creative therapies found that they had gained insight, and found that making things with their own hands was very cathartic. There is a wide range of art therapy categories to choose from, including dramatic, dance, music, literary, and poetry. This type of therapy can take place in a variety of settings: inpatient, outpatient, indoors or outdoors, and individual or group type settings. However, it is up to the therapist which setting would work best for their patient.

Psychodrama

Therapists have also found that role-playing and reconstructions of the patient's trauma can be a powerful intervention tool. Psychodrama gives patients a feeling of cathartic release and increased objectivity. It also gives the patient an understanding of how important a community of their peers is.

Drawing a Life-Sized Silhouette or Timeline

Drawing a timeline or a life-sized silhouette and sharing it in group therapy gives a multi-faceted effect for the patient, including: disclosing their truth, challenging their distorted thoughts, revealing patterns in their behavior, addressing their trauma and shame, developing a narrative about their life that is congruent to the truth, and proactively encouraging relapse prevention.

The Eight Essential Processes

Creative arts help evoke essential processes that are required for the patient's wellness and recovery. The eight essential processes can be used in either one structured session or a long-term treatment plan.

Authenticity

Art is used as a way to identify, explore, and express your emotions with realness and integrity. It uses lines, texture, color, tone, form, rhythm and flow, shapes, and movement to express your painful memories and feelings. As your artwork becomes congruent with your thoughts and emotions, you will start to feel empowered.

Catharsis

Art created during therapy can be used to discover a symbol that represents the person's inner world and thoughts. When you find this symbol, a feeling of relief will wash over you.

Projection

Projection is a therapeutic art piece that is used for self-reflection. It is a process to help people bypass the distortions in their cognitive thinking and gain some insight into who they truly are.

Sublimation

Sublimation means venting one's pain. For trauma survivors and people in recovery from addiction, art therapy provides a safe place for you to channel your negative energy into your creativity rather than using it against yourself or other people. It models a creative process for releasing negative energy, instead of a destructive one. An example would be someone who self-harms uses a felt-tip marker to draw lines or emotions on their body where they would normally cut or burn themselves.

Balancing Locus of Control

This essential process teaches you that you have a choice in how you respond to situations, giving you control of your destiny. Attention to locus control helps you determine what you can control and the ability to accept what you cannot change.

Identify Developmental Ego-States

This essential process is used to identify and honor your ego. When an adult that experiences trauma enters therapy, it is not uncommon for them to have built a bridge to a version of their younger self that experienced the trauma. Art therapy helps heal both sides of that bridge.

Integration

This essential process helps the patient identify all of the separated parts of themselves and bring them back together. This is done with art therapy by the symbolic use of color, textures, materials, and other media. The ultimate goal of this task is to develop balance, maturity, and a feeling of wholeness.

Transcendence

The process of transcendence gives the patient the ability to transform themselves and others through a spiritual connection to their 'Higher Power' or some form of a higher source. Producing art is a well-documented way of causing the artist to experience hypnotic states or an altered state of consciousness. This hypnotic state gives the patient a way of crossing into other realms of discovering their inner self, a collective unconsciousness, or God, depending on what the person's spiritual orientation is. Transcendence helps the patient accept how the world works, even in their darkest times.

Chapter 13:

Compassion and Forgiveness...

You Owe it To Yourself

Take David's Story

David used to beat himself up mentally and physically while he was using drugs and re-enacting his trauma. He found that compassion cut through all of the self-hatred and made a mental note to embrace that compassion every day. He knew that in order to be nicer to himself he would have to practice, and since he tended to be harsh with himself often, it gave him a lot of time to practice throughout the day. David finds ways to challenge himself to have and maintain a compassionate mindset, even when life gets hard.

Why Do You Need Compassion?

Finding true compassion allows you to finally forgive yourself, stop the blame, and learn how to understand who you are. It's not as simple as it sounds though, because the true test of compassion is whether or not it helps you change your unsafe and risky behavior. If you have compassion but your behavior doesn't change, it means that your compassion isn't authentic.

An Example of Compassion Toward Yourself

A good example of compassion toward yourself would be knowing and acknowledging your family's history of alcoholism despite wanting to drink and reminding yourself that you know that it isn't safe for you.

You know that your friends are allowed to drink, and it seems unfair at times. So instead of drinking, you allow yourself to have a different kind of treat that doesn't involve unhealthy behaviors.

True Compassion

Compassion isn't just saying nice and positive things to yourself daily. Recovery and true compassion sometimes require you to sacrifice or deprive yourself of the things that you love. Turning down a drink when you are craving it after a hard day shows compassion. Leaving a violent and cruel partner that you have been with for years shows compassion. Your choice may not be the easiest one, but it is the one that is best for you. Psychologist Kristen Neff states that, "having compassion for oneself entails desiring health and well-being for oneself, which means gently encouraging change where needed and rectifying harmful or unproductive patterns of behavior. Thus, self-compassion should counteract complacency" (Jacobsen et al., 2001).

What Compassion Is Not

To know and understand what true compassion is, you must know what compassion is not. True compassion is not

- Not taking responsibility for your mistakes.

- Pretending everything is fine when it isn't.

- Pity and selfishness.

- Trying to justify your bad choices.

- Being arrogant.

- Making excuses for your behavior.

Compassion Toward Yourself

You may find that it is a lot easier to be compassionate toward other people than it is to yourself, especially if you have trauma-related and addiction problems. It may even seem that being hard or harsh with yourself is considered to be normal. People that have been mistreated throughout their life tend to lean toward self-hate rather than encouragement. It could also go the opposite way, with the person being so arrogant that they think they could do no wrong. Over-loving and hating yourself are two sides of the same coin; however, people that are secure with their sense of self keep the awareness of their weaknesses and strengths balanced.

The only way to make a complete and real change is to balance your self-love and your limits. It's easy to feel stuck if you are always too hard on yourself. Or if you are constantly going back and forth between being too indulgent and too harsh. You get stuck, act out with one of your unhealthy behaviors, overindulge in it, feel bad for doing it, and then the cycle repeats itself all over again. Finding compassion with yourself is the only way to stop the cycle and feel balanced.

Note: To see where you stand, feel free to take the Self-Compassion Scale available at www.self-compassion.org/test-how-self-compassionateyou-are. It's a free, valid scale you can do anonymously online to see how compassionate you are toward yourself.

Forgive Yourself

Addiction and trauma have a way of leading you down a dark path filled with guilt, shame, and self-hatred. It becomes part of your nature to turn on yourself when you have been treated badly your entire life. The true meaning of forgiving yourself requires you to acknowledge and accept what happened to you, then take that experience and consciously learn from it to better your future. Acknowledging and accepting what happened doesn't make it right, acceptable, or that it won't happen again. It also doesn't mean that you forgive those who hurt you, it just means that you understand your part in the events leading you to get hurt. True forgiveness means that you let go of all the resentment you have toward yourself, show some self-respect, and allow yourself to move forward.

How: Feel the Forgiveness

You have to allow yourself to feel the forgiveness. You have to be able to let go of what you did or didn't do and accept it. Allow yourself to take your own side in the situation, and show yourself some compassion. Align yourself with the vulnerable side of you, the hurt side. Be there for yourself, even if no one else is. Accept the truth of what happened, and allow yourself to feel the pain. It may feel like too much to handle at first, but forgiving yourself will help the pain melt away.

How: Help Others

Sometimes people find it helpful to move forward with their lives by contributing their time and energy to help other people to make right what they have done wrong. If this is something that interests you, try to find a mission or task that is meaningful to you and your life. For example, if you are an animal lover, you might enjoy volunteering your time at your local humane society. Just make sure that when taking this approach that you stay balanced in your motives. Don't allow yourself to become more focused on your atonement that you lose sight of your goals.

How: Apologize

Knowing that you have hurt others may make forgiving yourself difficult. Apologizing to the people that you have hurt can make this process easier. Making amends to the people that you have wronged makes you accountable for your actions, and can help you move forward more smoothly. Once you have made your amends to the people that you have hurt, let go of the guilt and try not to dwell on your mistake anymore. The people to whom you apologize don't want to see you drowning in your self-pity and hatred because you hurt them, they want to see action. They want to see that you learned from

your mistakes and are doing your best to change your life around for
the better.

Chapter 14:

Get Good Coping Skills

Take Briana's Story

Briana was exposed to horrific trauma when she was a young girl. In order to fill the emptiness that she felt inside, she filled her closet with clothes and other things that she didn't need. She was addicted to purchasing and owning material items, until one day she realized that the stuff she had on the outside would not fill the empty hole she felt on the inside. Unfortunately, Briana didn't learn this lesson until she had created a devastating financial situation. Her coping skill was unsafe and it was causing her a lot of pain, emotionally and financially. Once Briana learned what safe and healthy coping skills were, she could start to heal. Healing for her meant that she needed to understand that she had a choice on how she reacted to what happened in the world around her. Briana stopped placing the blame on other people for the mess she had created and took responsibility for her unsafe coping skill. Her financial ruin caused her to lose her car, giving her no choice but to take the bus back and forth to work. She didn't take her time on the bus for granted though, because every day for six months she would look at the list of healthy coping skills that she made and pick one to use that day.

Choose Good Coping

Coping means how you respond to your problems and how you solve those problems. Going through a painful experience, like a divorce, may cause you to choose unhealthy coping skills to help you deal with the emotional pain. Poor coping skills would include drinking excessively, isolating yourself, and overindulging in junk food. These coping skills may seem to help solve your problems, but they are short-term fixes that can turn into long-term problems. Long-term healthy coping skills would be managing your self-care, getting enough sleep, exercising, or joining support groups.

Good coping strategies cannot start without accepting the fact that you can't always have control over what happens around you, but you do have control over how you react. Look for positive solutions that build up your strength and healing. As long as what you are doing isn't hurting yourself or others, it is a good coping skill. Addiction and trauma can make it difficult to find healthy coping skills, but it is possible to learn.

Explore . . . The Safe Coping Skills List

Make a list of some safe coping skills. Just remember that context matters, as the setting for some coping skills is not appropriate for others. Good examples of some safe coping skills include

- Reaching out to someone when you need help.

- Knowing when to leave a situation when it starts to feel dangerous.

- Carrying around an item that inspires you.

- Never giving up and being persistent.

- Showing yourself some compassion.

- Trying new and innovative ways to solve problems.

- Making time to take care of yourself.

- Setting healthy boundaries and learning how to say no.

- Letting yourself cry, it's nothing to be ashamed of.

- Choosing honesty and self-respect.

- Organizing your life. To-do lists make life seem manageable and controllable.

- Going over a negative event carefully, and figuring out what you would do differently next time.

- Noticing the cost of the addiction.

- Carefully thinking over the consequences of your choices.

- Accepting all the parts of yourself.

- Replacing your destructive activities with something fun and healthy (new hobbies, crafts, etc.).

- Focusing on the present, without getting hung up on the past or the future.

- Making a specific plan and putting it into action.

- Building a wall to protect yourself from negative or dangerous people.

- Attending some type of treatment or meeting (AA, counseling, group therapy).

- Trying something new and interesting every day.

- Remembering that being alone is better than being in a toxic relationship. Even casual hookups can set you up to restart the cycle of unsafe or risky behaviors that you are trying to avoid.

- Remind yourself why you are working so hard if you start to feel stuck. Are you doing it for your kids? For your spouse? For your health?

Chapter 15:

Breaking Harmful Family Coping

Patterns

Take Jade's Story

Jade was severely neglected as a child and was forced to learn everything on her own due to her parent's absence. Unfortunately, she wasn't taught by her essential caregivers that becoming successful in life was a continual effort. With the false belief that people are supposed to be happy and feel good all the time, Jade started taking drugs in middle school. She didn't know how to be happy and feel good all the time, and drugs helped her do that—until they didn't. Jade's parents weren't drug addicts, living on the street, forcing her to be alone all the time while they got their next score. They were wealthy and successful entrepreneurs and functioning alcoholics. Their constant preaching about the need of keeping up appearances and not allowing yourself to be vulnerable left Jade unable to trust other people. She had difficulty figuring out how to let go of her childhood feelings of shame, guilt, awkwardness, and fear. Her parent's perseverance in the workplace helped her become successful in business, but her emotional availability in her relationships was stunted.

Break the Cycle

The biggest predictor of both trauma and addiction problems is one's family history. Having relatives in your family that have addiction problems, makes you more susceptible to having one yourself. The same thing goes for trauma, if your family has a history of trauma, you are more likely to be exposed to trauma as well. This cycle is commonly known as intergenerational addiction and trauma: a cycle that is passed down through generations until someone goes through recovery in order to stop it.

You can be the one to break the cycle by making recovery your priority. Many children that grew up with parents that were alcoholics don't have substance abuse problems, and many of them that grew up abused don't grow up to abuse their own children. Why? Because they learned from their parent's mistakes and took the precautionary measures needed and made recovery an important part of their life.

Be Aware of the Message You Absorbed and Put You at Risk

One of the best ways to break this cycle is by becoming aware of the messages you heard when you were a child. You may be unaware that you absorbed that message, it was just a part of your life. These messages create rules within the household that are needed for the child to survive, creating a powerful force field around your home that would silence them.

Messages that play a part in your addiction may include

- You are only worth as much money as you have.

- Food equals love.

- Drinking is the best way to relax after a hard day.

- Live for today, not tomorrow.

Messages that play a part in your trauma may include

- Don't show your emotions or appear vulnerable.

- Pretend like everything is okay.

- Your needs and feelings don't matter.

- Violence is normal for everyone.

- I would never lie to you.

- You will never see me again if you tell.

- I will give you something to cry about.

- Stop begging for attention.

Where Do These Messages Come From?

These messages were ones that you learned as a child. They may have come from your parents, friends, media, your school, or even your culture. You may be aware of some of the messages and their origins, but there are some you may not be aware of. Most of the time the cultural messages that you have absorbed happen subconsciously because many cultures value different things. Some value personal expression versus conformity, or equality versus power.

Why Do They Matter to You Now?

Each of these messages is a building block of who you become as an adult. They lay the foundation for the choices you make, your likes and dislikes, what you can tolerate, your values, and how you communicate with others. The messages can change over time, and some you may choose to reject. Some messages may be a negative influence on you, while some may be a positive influence. However, some of these messages may be so extreme that they are considered to be unhealthy and restrict how much you can adapt to varying situations. Flexibility is an essential and healthy survival skill.

Explore . . . Choose the Messages You Want to Keep

Choosing what messages you want to keep in your life can help you create the life you want, and see how those messages will affect your life. Take the unhealthy messages you absorbed as a child and replace them with healthy ones you want to live by as an adult. For example:

- Turn "don't trust people" into "there are people that are trustworthy."

- Turn "eat your feelings" into "express your feelings."

- Turn "take what you get" into "ask for the things you want."

- Turn "drinking helps solve your problems" into "alcohol isn't a solution."

- Turn "you aren't as important as other people" into "you are as important as others."

- Turn "only look out for yourself" into "we can all work together."

- Turn "addiction is a choice" into "addiction is a mental illness."

- Turn "don't talk about your issues" into "issues need to be aired out and resolved."

- Turn "children should only talk when they are spoken to" into "children should be free to express themselves how they please."

- Turn "everyone else has it together, but me" into "everyone struggles eventually."

- Turn "life only brings you stress" into "you should enjoy your life."

- Turn "you will never amount to anything" into "I can go as far as I want to."

Explore Messages From Outside Your Family

Take a broader view and explore where these negative messages came from. Think of your earlier experiences and influences. Were your earlier influences the media, your community, your culture, or your family history? Was it from people outside of your family? Once you realize what influenced you, you can feel more compassion for how those messages put you where you are today. Don't judge yourself, just gain some insight. Your insight will help remind you that there are reasons for the problems that you have with addiction and trauma.

Chapter 16:

Grounding

Take Rita's Story

Rita is an Army veteran. The Army did its job and taught her how to be army-strong, unable to feel emotions, and just act on her training. She was at the top of her class and was well-respected by her fellow soldiers, with most of them being men. She held her own during training and could keep up with them at the bar as well. Drinking heavily at the bar was considered the norm where she was stationed. If something good, bad, or indifferent happened, the soldiers would drink. Until one night, Rita had too much to drink and was sexually assaulted by a man in her unit. After that night, her drinking became a way to deal with her emotional pain and rage. Knowing that she would be blamed for the assault because she had been drinking, she never reported her assault. Rita tried to keep her life together, but it seemed impossible. She kept drinking to the point of inebriation, even getting arrested for hitting a parked car and driving under the influence. She was sent to the military hospital for psychiatric care, and it was there that she learned how the trauma from her sexual assault turned her favorite pastime into a serious drinking problem. Alcohol put her in autopilot mode, made her feel numb, and made her unable to feel the pain from her attack. In treatment, Rita was taught how to focus on the outside world to regain her sense of control and stay grounded in the present moment.

What Is Grounding?

Grounding is an acquired skill that helps you stay on top of your emotions and make a habit of managing them. Having feelings makes us human, and all feelings are normal. However, when you have a history of trauma or addiction, sometimes those feelings can be overwhelming or make you feel numb. This skill was first developed and used in psychiatric hospitals with the main purpose of helping trauma survivors who were considered a danger to themselves and others. Grounding helped them regain a sense of control and feel calmer.

Many people find that most of their unsafe and unhealthy behaviors happen when they feel stuck in their heads. Grounding helps bring you back to the present. It means to focus on the world around you, rather than the negative feelings in order to gain a sense of peace. Think of it as a lifeline or a lifejacket, keeping you afloat when giant waves of emotions hit you unexpectedly. It also allows your body to calm itself down, while sending messages to your brain that there isn't a real, imminent threat to your safety at that time. Ironically, the messages being sent to your brain help you get out of your head, as you are reminded to refocus your attention and slow down. There are three types of grounding methods that will be discussed in the 'Explore' section of this chapter: physical, soothing, and mental.

When Can You Use It?

You can use grounding methods and techniques anytime and anywhere. You can use them before, during, and after a distressing situation. They are particularly helpful for when you start to feel any negative or overwhelming emotions such as anger, anxiety, sadness, panic, fear, dissociation, urges and cravings, stress, or when you feel triggered. Grounding techniques are simple, but powerful, and are an important skill in recovery.

How Do People Usually Learn Grounding?

Children from healthy families learn how to ground when their emotional needs are met consistently, like being comforted when they are upset or in distress. The child also learns how to manage their emotions properly by watching their parents and other people in the home. Unfortunately, not everyone was lucky enough to be born in a healthy, emotionally available family. These are the children that learned how to shift away and avoid their negative feelings. They are the ones that have difficulty self-soothing as adults and have become so accustomed to feeling distressed that it has become second nature to them.

Having a healthy sense of detachment doesn't mean becoming numb to your feelings or not caring about anything, including yourself. It entails staying in the moment, being present, calm, and centered. Mindful meditation and relaxation are just a couple of examples of the various methods you can use to accomplish a feeling of being present. However, these grounding methods were not designed to reduce your cravings or impulses but rather to put you in a calmer state of mind so that you can deal with them. Grounding is more effective than other approaches and can be accomplished by increasing your awareness of the world around you.

Explore . . . Try Grounding

As previously stated, grounding can be done anytime and anywhere, like on the bus, in the grocery store, or at school. The best part about this method is that nobody has to know that you are doing it. Doing it when you are in distress or dissociating puts a distance between you and the trigger that caused the negative feelings. Keep yourself in the moment by keeping your eyes open, scanning the environment around you, and avoid thinking about the past or the future. Before and after you do this technique, be sure to rate the intensity of your emotions or mood on a scale of zero to ten, with ten being the most stress you ever felt in your life. Stay neutral about your thoughts, don't judge whether the thoughts are good or bad.

There are four steps to the grounding technique that you can use to practice as a reference for which grounding method will work for you when overwhelming negative feelings arise.

Step 1: Think of something or an event that you find to be moderately distressing. The event doesn't have to be the worst thing you can think of, but something that brings a feeling of discomfort, preferably a five or seven on your distress scale.

Step 2: Honestly rate the chosen thought or event on the distress scale with zero being no distress, and ten being the most intense. The reason for this rating is to see which grounding method works for you and how well it works.

Step 3: Use as many methods as you can for at least ten minutes, in any order that you choose. Just do the methods—no judgments and no comments needed.

Step 4: After using some of these methods, rate your distress level once more. Did the rating level go down, even just a small amount? Are you feeling a little bit better than before you used some of these methods? If not, try again for another ten minutes, this time using different methods than you used the first time. See which one(s) works best for you.

Physical Grounding Methods

Physical grounding techniques are used so that you can get out of your head and refocus on what is happening to your body and what is going on in your surroundings. Focusing on objects around you or how your body feels when you do a certain action cancels out your negative thoughts and lowers your distress level.

- Run your hands under cold or warm water.

- Tightly squeeze an object around you and consciously notice what it feels like. For example: is the object soft, fluffy, hard, sticky?

- Touch different objects around the room: your clothing, keys, a pencil, the walls, the table. Notice textures, colors, materials, weight, temperature. Compare the different objects' colors, textures, weights, and materials.

- "Ground" or dig your heels into the floor or carpet. Take a mental note on how the tension in your heels makes you feel physically centered.

- Carry around a chosen grounding object in your pocket. It can be a small object, like a small rock, a ring, a piece of clay, or a piece of yarn, that you can touch whenever you start to feel triggered.

- Jump up and down on the ground.

- Take a bite of a lemon or something sour. Take note of the sour food's texture, color, and smell. A lemon is the best suggestion because you can use all of your senses, and the smell and taste are hard to ignore.

- Pet an animal. Focus on how the animal's fur feels between your fingers as you brush through it.

- Move your body. Stretch, do a dance, do some yoga. Focus your attention on how your body feels during each motion.

Soothing Grounding Methods

The best time to use soothing grounding methods is in times of extreme distress. They are used to comfort you and help the positive emotions to take over the negative ones.

- Speak kindly to your inner child: "You will get through this because you are strong and brave."

- Think of a list of your favorite things: favorite season, animal, color, food, quote, TV show, person, place, activity, movie, time of day, song lyrics, and smell.

- Look at pictures of the people that you care about: your children, grandparents, or best friends.

- Say the words to an inspiring song, poem, prayer, or quote that makes you feel better.

- Think of a safe place and describe why you find it safe and soothing.

- Create or repeat a memorable coping statement. For example, "I can handle this" or "This too shall pass."

- Think of something that you are looking forward to in the next week, like spending time with a friend or going to a concert.

- Cuddle with a pet. Animals have a strange way of knowing when we are overwhelmed, and they know their job is to make you feel better. Spending some quality time cuddling with your pet and taking a nap is perfect to soothe your discomforts.

- Listen to your favorite song or watch your favorite movie. It could be your favorite song or movie from your childhood or a happy time in your life. It doesn't matter how many times you have heard or watched it, just pretend like you are doing it for the first time.

Mental Grounding Methods

Mental grounding techniques are used to focus your negative thoughts in another direction. Counting, listing, or taking note of physical objects around you requires that you step away from your thoughts and pay attention to other things.

- Take note of the objects in your environment using all five of your senses. For example: "The room smells like lavender," "My comforter feels fluffy," "I hear the sound of the television," "The apples on the counter taste sweet," "I see the blue walls in my bedroom."

- Play a category game in your head. Think of different types of penguins, baseball players, state capitals, or words that start with A.

- Describe, in great detail, an everyday activity that you enjoy doing or that has a lot of steps. For example, describe the steps you need to do for the meal that you plan on cooking that night.

- Use your imagination and imagine how you would symbolically escape from the situation or your negative feelings.

- Create a safety statement that will remind you of who and where you are. For example: "My name is [your name] and I am safe right now. I am in the right here, in the present, not the past. I live in [your location] and the date is ..."

- Use some humor and think of a joke, read a book, or watch your favorite funny movie to bring yourself out of a bad mood.

- Play a memory game or a card game, like solitaire. These games require that you pay attention to what you are doing, and pull the attention away from your distressing emotions.

How to Boost Your Grounding

Like any skill, you need to practice the grounding techniques so that they become a powerful tool in your toolbelt. Try to use some of these boosting suggestions to make your grounding skill as strong as you possibly can.

- Practice as much as you possibly can, so that you can memorize your method.

- Try using grounding in different situations. For example, when someone cuts you off on the expressway, when you feel depressed or overwhelmed, or when you are having a hard time falling asleep.

- Practice speeding up the amount of time it takes you to focus on the outside world.

- Try grounding techniques for at least twenty to thirty minutes on repeat.

- Try to notice which of the three methods work out the best for you–soothing, mental, or physical grounding methods, or possibly a combination of the three.

- You can always create your own grounding methods. You never know, it may work better than any of the methods you have read, because you know yourself better than anyone else.

- Learn how to start grounding methods early on during a negative mood, at the beginning of a flashback, when you first have a craving to use, or when you feel your anger start to build up.

- Write down a list of your favorite grounding methods, and how long it takes for them to be effective when you are using them.

- Teach your family and friends about your grounding methods, and have them help you, or remind you when they notice you have become overwhelmed.

- Prepare, prepare, prepare. Locate different places in your home, at work, and in your car where you have your safety object or reminders for you to use grounding techniques.

- Tape a voice recording of a grounding message so that you can listen to it when you need to. You could ask your therapist or someone who brings you comfort, to record the message for you.

Chapter 17:

Relapse: Fall Again. Fall Better.

Take Maggie's Story

Maggie is a survivor of childhood sexual abuse, neglect, and domestic violence. She started to drink heavily as a teenager to deal with the memories of her trauma, leading her to deal with the pain of chronic pancreatitis when she got older. Going to the hospital every time she had a pancreatitis attack caused her a great amount of distress, making her feel like a child again. She would take out her pain on everyone around her at the hospital, her husband, and the nurses. She would throw child-like tantrums, or think about harming herself. With the help of her husband, therapist, and friends, Maggie started to feel the support she craved throughout her childhood. Maggie started to realize that there was no reason to panic every time she went to the hospital because every time she left there, she felt better. The love and support of her family and friends encouraged her to stay aware of how she was feeling and thinking, and she tried to stay in the present. Every day she reminds herself that her needs and wants are valid, no matter how big or small they are, and she responds to them with a newfound sense of compassion. Maggie also learned that she doesn't need to act out like a child anymore when her needs aren't met. She isn't in that unsafe environment anymore, so there is no need to yell to be heard. Maggie was able to abstain from alcohol completely, while she focused on healing from her traumatic past.

What's a Relapse?

A relapse is backsliding or moving back a few steps after a period of vast improvement. It is a minor setback, but you were so successful in reducing your negative behaviors, cravings, urges, and symptoms, that there should be no doubt in your mind that you can do it again. Relapse is a word that is usually associated with people that are recovering from drug addiction, but in all actuality, it can be any negative behavior that is dangerous to your progress. People sometimes use the word slip interchangeably with relapse, but they are not the same thing. Slip is just a tiny step backward, definitively less severe or intense as a full relapse. A perfect example would be if you have one drink, but you stop yourself from having another one and get right back on track with your recovery.

What to Do for an Addiction Relapse

Your vulnerability is at an all-time high right after a relapse. It is understandable how easy it would be for you to hate yourself for your actions, but berating yourself will only make you feel worse, possibly leading you to even more dangerous behaviors.

If you have an addiction relapse, try out a few of these suggestions to help get you back on track.

- If you backtrack, remember what lesson you have learned for the next time.

- Identify which of your needs are not being met. Having a relapse means that you needed something but weren't sure how to satisfy it safely. Learn how to listen closely to your needs and respond to them in healthy and safe ways

- Notice something in your life that is going right. Sometimes it is just a simple "I'm still alive." But that simple thing is your lifeline.

- Use your survival skills. Remember that in the wilderness, it is essential to stay calm, figure out a plan, think clearly and rationally, and stay hopeful that you will find your way out of the darkness.

- Don't wallow in self-pity. Prevent any further damage, and stop your relapse dead in its tracks as quickly as possible.

- Understand that relapse doesn't happen all at once. There are often a subtle set of changes or signs that slowly start to intensify or a build-up of patterns signaling that you are headed for a relapse. These signs could include feelings of increased stress, irritation, moodiness, tension, or boredom. There are also some physical signs, like stomach aches or a series of headaches. Do whatever you can to keep your mind busy and off of your urges, but stay aware of your patterns and signs.

- Imagine an instant replay of what happened, and figure out what coping skills could have worked for you before, during, or after a relapse in order to prevent it.

- Put off your self-blame for just a little while. Focus on the ability to stop your behavior right that second, then staying clean for an hour/day/week/month. By the end of that time, you will have focused so much on staying sober that you won't hate or blame yourself anymore.

- Realize that relapse is part of recovery for a lot of people with addiction and trauma-related problems. Eventually, one of your relapses will become your last. This may not be your first relapse, but it will hopefully be your last.

What to Do for a Relapse of Trauma Problems

All of the suggestions that can help you handle an addiction relapse can work for a relapse in your trauma problem too. A relapse in your trauma problems can be just as painful and real as an addiction relapse. Luckily, relapses for your trauma-related problems and symptoms are usually more subtle than an addiction relapse. There aren't risky or unsafe behaviors that could temporarily derail your progress, like drinking or gambling but trauma relapses, you could find that you have stepped back into a younger version of yourself. You could feel a child-like part of you take over when you feel panicked, afraid, or in an enormous amount of distress. Some people have even reported that they reverted to an extremely paranoid state of mind, while some feel like they are unable to take the age-appropriate measures in taking care of themselves.

Chapter 18:

Apps and Organizations to Help

Along the Way

There are various apps and government-funded organizations that can help you while you recover and afterward to help keep your life on track. Some of these resources are phone apps, information and support, hotlines, assessment tools, and referrals for treatment.

Trauma/PTSD

Apps Available on Your Phone

- T2 Mood Tracker

- PTSD Coach

- Circle of 6

- Mindshift

Organizations

- *National Center for PTSD*. This website was developed by the Veterans Affairs in order to provide resources for military veterans and people dealing with PTSD (www.ptsd.va.gov).

- *Adverse Childhood Experiences Study*. The ACES website provides information on how childhood neglect and abuse can make an impact on your adult life and includes a free online screening assessment (www.acesconnection.com).

- *Behavioral Health Treatment Locator.* This effective and useful online tool searches your area for treatment locations, provided by The Substance Abuse and Mental Health Services Administration (https://findtreatment.samhsa.gov/).

- *Anxiety and Depression Association of America.* The ADAA website provides information about PTSD and includes a free online screening assessment (https://adaa.org/screening-posttraumatic-stress-disorder-ptsd).

- *National Alliance on Mental Illness.* This NAMI-promoted website provides people that are looking for resources, referrals, and support for their mental illnesses, including PTSD (www.nami.org).

- *National Child Traumatic Stress Network.* This website can provide information for families, children, and teens that have been affected by childhood trauma (www.nctsn.org).

- *National Resource Center on Domestic Violence.* This website can provide you with information on the treatment and prevention of domestic violence (www.nrcdv.org).

Hotlines

- *National Domestic Violence Hotline.* This helpline is available 24 hours a day, 7 days a week, 365 days a year for victims of domestic violence.

  Their toll-free number is: (1-800) 779-7233 (www.thehotline.org).

- *National Disaster Distress Helpline.* This crisis support helpline is promoted by The Substance Abuse and Mental Health Services Administration, to help people from communities that have been personally affected by tornadoes, earthquakes, tsunamis, etc.

Their toll-free number is: (1-800) 985-5990 (www.samhsa.gov/find-help/disaster-distress-helpline).

Addiction/Substance Abuse

Apps

- AlcoDroid (free drink counter)

- MYGU (monitors gambling cravings)

Organizations

- 12-Step Treatment Programs. There are multiple local and telephone support groups for every type of addiction program that uses the 12-Step program: For addictions to gambling (www.gamblersanonymous.org), teens amid their own drug or alcohol addictions (www. teen-anon.com), overspending (www.debtorsanonymous.org), nicotine (www.nicotine-anonymous.org), sex addiction (www.sa.org), overeating (www.oa.org), cocaine (www.ca.org), narcotics (www.na.org), alcoholism (www.aa.org), and for family members that need support during their loved one's recovery (www.al-anon.org).

- *National Council on Alcoholism and Drug Dependence.* This website provides referrals and information for people, and their families, struggling with substance abuse (www.ncadd.org).

- *National Institute on Alcohol Abuse and Alcoholism.* This website provides information for people, and their families, struggling with alcohol abuse (www.niaaa.nih.gov).

- *Harm Reduction Coalition.* This organization's website can provide information on how to prevent a drug overdose and decrease the stigma for drug abusers that are trying to get help (www.harmreduction.org).

- *Vet Change.* This website provides military veterans with self-help tools and information about PTSD and alcohol or substance abuse (www.vetchange.org).

- *Rethinking Drinking.* This website is promoted by the National Institute on Alcohol Abuse and Alcoholism and provides multiple interactive tools, including: how to monitor your alcohol use, identifying if you may have a drinking problem, and treatment referrals if it is needed (www.rethinkingdrinking.niaaa.nih.gov).

- *SMART Recovery.* This organization is a self-help group that provides help similar to AA, but takes a non-spiritual approach. Their website provides a list of online and local groups that follow their approach (www.smartrecovery.org).

- *National Institute on Drug Abuse.* This website provides an enormous amount of information on drug abuse (www.nida.nih.gov).

Hotline

- *National Helpline.* This helpline was created by the Substance Abuse and Mental Health Services Administration and is available 24 hours a day, 7 days a week, 365 days a year for people that are seeking information or treatment referrals for mental illness and substance abuse.

  Their toll-free number is: (1-800) 662-HELP (4357) (www.samhsa.gov/find-help/national-helpline)

Suicide Prevention

Apps

- A Friend Asks

- Operation Reach Out

- MY3

- Stay Alive

Organizations

- *American Foundation for Suicide Prevention.* This organization's website provides life-saving education and advocates for suicide prevention (www.afsp.org).

Hotline

- *National Suicide Prevention Lifeline.* This hotline is available 24 hours a day, 7 days a week, 365 days a year for people that are suicidal or contemplating suicide and require immediate resources or someone to talk to.

  Their toll-free number is: (1-800) 273-TALK (8255) (www.suicidepreventionlifeline.org)

Chapter 19:

Living a Good Life

The right question is whether we as a society need people who have emerged from some kind of trauma—and the answer is that we plainly do. This is not a pleasant fact to contemplate. For every remote miss who becomes stronger, there are countless near misses who are crushed by what they have been through. There are times and places, however, when all of us depend on people who have been hardened by their experiences. –Malcolm Gladwell

Sometimes it is hard to imagine a total recovery after a life full of hardship and pain. Living a happy, healthy, and full life is possible though. Maybe reading over some stories of real people that have been exactly where you are in your journey will open your eyes, so you can see that this is just the beginning. You are strong and brave, and you can get through this process with your head held high and compassion in your heart. Just remember that you have already come this far and have survived the worst of it, so why would you want to stop now?

Jillian's Recovery

Jillian struggled with her mental health and substance abuse since she was a teenager. She was never diagnosed with an anxiety disorder or chronic depression, but she would take whatever pills she could get her hands on to make herself feel better. As time went on, her self-medicating and self-destructive behaviors only got worse. She had normally stuck with using one substance at a time, and some years were better than others, depending on how she was feeling during that time. Throughout her years of substance abuse, she was able to abstain from using for months, on one occasion up to a year at a time, but would always end up relapsing.

As she moved into adulthood, she found that she had a growing interest in working with support and outreach programs. Her passion led her to work with patients dealing with addiction, trauma, pain, and depression. It wasn't until years of working with her patients and seeing multiple counselors that Jillian discovered that she had PTSD, possibly even Complex Post-Traumatic Disorder (C-PTSD) stemming from her childhood trauma. Her work with the outreach program had become a trigger for her symptoms and had increased in their intensity. After years of counseling, Jillian can now clearly see that her need to self-medicate was actually just the need to feel numb. She knows that addiction is a chronic progressive disease, and the longer she ignored her problems, the worse her addiction got. Jillian knows from experience that recovery is an ongoing process, and there is a significant difference between just abstaining from using and making a full recovery from addiction and trauma. She can clearly see the factors that led to her using drugs in the first place, and why she filled the void of her unmet needs with substances rather than getting the help she deserved. To Jillian, recovery means facing her triggers head-on, healing her damaged inner child, and move forward with her life so she can be comfortable in her own skin.

Chan's Recovery

Chan was cursed with the gift of intergenerational trauma, with the previous generations of his family passing along their pain and trauma down to him. He grew up with frequent bouts of abuse and hostility from his mother and grandmother, leading to an immense amount of self-hatred and self-doubt. He was in constant conflict with himself, wrestling with his self-worth, what was real versus what he was told, and feelings of inadequacy. His feelings of worthlessness and self-loathing created the perfect storm, pushing him down the path of serious drug addiction.

He learned early on in treatment that time and patience are virtues in the healing process. Years after ending his long-term addiction to methamphetamines and entering a recovery program, Chan found that he was still struggling with Post-Acute Withdrawal Syndrome. He showed all of the classic symptoms: trouble concentrating, foggy memory, empty stares, and blank thoughts. He felt broken and worried that the damage that he had done to his brain from years of using may never heal. Chan was infuriated at how much of his life drugs had stolen from him, including his memories, rational thoughts, and his mind's ability to work at its previous capabilities. Today, Chan is proud to say that he has been sober for three years, but his brain has yet to catch up with his recovery. He has been able to do some serious work on himself, reflecting on his past and how much of his trauma had to do with his drug use. It was difficult for him to open up about his trauma and addiction at first, but once he came to terms with the cause and effects of his past, he became comfortable talking about it to anyone looking for help.

Matt's Recovery

Matt was in his sophomore year in college when his struggles of becoming successful in life and his inability to cope with difficult situations came to a head. He was ridiculed as a young child for being small and a late bloomer, but made up for his size and insecurities with extreme aggression. He channeled that anger into something logical, ice hockey. He excelled at the sport, but decided to quit after high school when he realized he would never be good enough to be on a professional team. Matt moved to New Orleans for college and transferred his focus from playing hockey to partying hard. He was determined to party harder and drink more than anyone at every party, often adding drugs to his regimen a few nights a week. He considered it to be normal behavior for a college kid. He was still able to function in school, despite his drug use and drinking, for about 18 months. His grades were slowly dropping, but he found other ways around failing so he could stay in school. In the winter of his sophomore year, he woke up to find out that his best friend had died in a car accident the night before. The news hit him hard, and he was not equipped to deal with the emotions that came with it. That all changed when he was offered some oxytocin to take the edge off.

Matt was in love with the drug after the first time he used it, wondering why he had never tried it before. He felt euphoric and all of his painful emotions about his friend's passing had melted away. That first try turned into weeks of consistent use, but it was no longer to ease his pain about the loss of his friend. It was all about catching the next high for him. Within a few months, Matt wasn't even the same person anymore. He had become an addict, a thief, and a liar. He was no longer a functional and occasional drug user or drinker and years later, his addiction was completely out of control.

He will never forget Valentine's Day in 2012 when a friend that was worried about him reached out and asked him to get help. Matt realized that his friend was right to be worried, and went to sleep that night intending to come clean to his parents the next morning. He did just that, and within a few short hours, he was on his way to Lubbock, Texas for treatment. After an agonizing detox, every day started to get better. With the help of the treatment center's staff, Matt was able to cut through the thick layers of his years-long addiction with the takeaway that his recovery is something that he would have to work on for the rest of his life. He continued with the skills and tools he was taught at treatment and decided to continue his education at the Center for the Study of Addiction and Recovery located at Texas Tech University. Matt graduated in January 2014, and today he is living in Manhattan, New York where he works with people that are in the same position that he once found himself in.

Marc's Recovery

Marc didn't have it easy growing up. He struggled in school, finding it difficult to string simple words together while he tried to read. He eventually found out that he had a severe form of a learning disability called dyslexia. Marc's peers considered his trouble with reading an invitation to bully him incessantly, making him feel like even more of an outcast.

His friends pressured him into drinking a beer and smoking a cigarette during his teenage years, but he didn't like either of them. He hated the taste, and they weren't a good experience for him. A few years later, he tried both of them again and was much happier with his experience. He found that he actually liked the taste of hard liquor more than beer. He started smoking and drinking daily until he discovered how good he felt when he used cocaine.

The first time he used cocaine definitely wasn't the last, and his addiction quickly spiraled out of control. He was in and out of rehabilitation centers between the ages of 17–19 When driving under the influence of drugs, Marc was in a near-fatal car accident, leaving him technically dead for almost three minutes and in a coma for two days. He came out of his coma with a cracked skull, and three metal plates holding the pieces of his face together. Walking away from his car accident alive made Marc feel like he was invincible, driving him to use drugs even more. The day that he got out of jail after a year-long stint, he went right back to using cocaine again.

He moved around from city to city, but the change of scenery didn't seem to change his behavior. Marc eventually got a union job and married a woman who had her own issues with addiction. They had a child together a couple of years later, and Marc distracted himself from his own issues by trying to take care of his wife's alcoholism and eating disorder. Neither Marc nor his wife was happy and they knew something had to change, so they filed for divorce and went to separate treatment centers in different states.

Marc found religion in treatment, but when he got out, he didn't follow his 12-step program and relapsed into using oxycontin and crack cocaine. He then moved on to methadone and roxies, while still keeping up with his addiction to cocaine. He lost custody of his baby, who was sent to live with Marc's family members. His shame and self-pity made his addiction spiral out of control even more. Until one day, Marc's brother bought him a one-way ticket to a treatment center in Arizona. His two-day bus ride gave him time to think about his life and his kid, and when he arrived at the treatment center, he decided to take it seriously this time.

Today, Marc has been sober for over a year and hasn't used cocaine in over 18 months. He has made a complete change and now spends his time as a sponsor trying to help others get clean and change their lives.

Ashley's Recovery

Looking back on her childhood, Ashley knows that it wasn't normal. Her family didn't have much, but then again, neither did many of her friends' families. Besides the lack of funds in the household, there was also a lack of goodnight hugs and bedtime stories. Instead, her bedtime routine consisted of praying that the sound of her mom and her mother's boyfriend fighting and screaming at each other didn't wake up her baby brother. She lay in bed at night listening to them and wondering how she would get to the phone if the screaming turned into a violent altercation. She dreamed about her father coming back, but when she woke up, she wondered how long he would stick around before he left again.

Learning how to maintain a toxic relationship isn't the only thing that Ashley learned from her parents. She learned that when her feelings got too overwhelming, you could push them down until you couldn't feel them anymore. If pushing the feelings down didn't work there was another alternative—get drunk and do drugs. Ashley got drunk for the first time at a young age, when a family member offered her alcohol.

Ashley remembered always being sent to the school nurse when she was in elementary school, often complaining of stomach aches but was always sent back to class with her tummy issues quickly dismissed. She didn't realize until years later, while in recovery, that she was already suffering from the symptoms of chronic stress and PTSD. The toxicity of her stress created a pattern of substance abuse, as she tried to find any way possible to escape from the realities of her chaotic home life. The drugs relieved the emotional pain and her anxiety was numbed. They stopped her nightmares and constant dread of accidentally telling someone about what was happening at home. Growing up and moving onto romantic relationships of her own, she found that all of them were as toxic as her parent's relationships. However, instead of fighting all the time, she changed every detail about herself to keep her partner happy.

Everything changed one day when she woke up in a jail cell with no recollection of what happened. She was ashamed of herself and made a call that would change her life. She found the will to live, and that was her first official day of recovery. Ashley has now been in recovery for years, and she doesn't take one day for granted. The road to recovery wasn't always smooth, but she kept going and kept moving forward. Ashley took one major lesson from her journey: that it's okay to look back on your past, as long as you keep going toward your future.

Your Own Successful Recovery Story

As you can see, all of these people have a past that led them down the wrong path. And the path that led them to use drugs and alcohol was only the beginning, as there are many winding roads filled with destructive behaviors and hurt loved ones that are left behind. Even after your recovery, there is damage control that needs to be done, apologies to be made, and relationships that need to be repaired.

Writing your own successful recovery story can inspire others, showing them that you have been in the same place that they are right now and you made it through to see another day. Your personal story can connect with someone in the same predicament as you once were, as they try to sort out their emotions stemming from the events of their traumatic past and what led them to this particular point in their lives. It shows the people that are looking for a glimmer of hope that you once also felt alone and hopeless, but through perseverance and emotional resilience you realized just the opposite—you were not alone or hopeless, and you found people that loved you and supported you in your recovery process.

Your recovery is unique, just like the journey it took you to get there. Writing your story can be cathartic, help you let go, and take responsibility for your recovery. It gives you permission to look back on your past and appreciate how far you have come, deepening your sense of self-awareness. Your narrative will strengthen your grasp on the reality that you have something to offer other people, like hope, compassion, and forgiveness. Remember to take some of those qualities and extend them to yourself too.

What lies behind us and what lies before us are tiny matters compared to what lies within us. –Ralph Waldo Emerson

Conclusion

As you can now see, childhood trauma is a significant contributor to the patterns of substance abuse. However, now that you are informed that recovery is, in fact, achievable, it is time to have the better life that you want and deserve. Hopefully, the most important thing that you remember, or your main takeaway, from reading this book is that what happened to you is not your fault by any means. You did not deserve what happened to you, and you didn't deserve to go through the pain that it caused you. You may not have control of the world around you, but you can control how you react to it. Without the guidance or support from the people that were supposed to have your best interest at heart, how else were you supposed to express your feelings about what happened? The bottled emotions that you pushed down for years only intensified the possibility of explosive destruction, destroying anything and everything in its path.

You may not have been blessed with a healthy and stable family, but that doesn't mean that you can't have one now. You know through your experiences what not to do, and by putting your best foot forward, you can create the life you have always dreamed of. You can learn how to use healthy coping skills, forgive yourself, find some compassion for your younger self so that you can move on with your life. You can lay the foundation over your resolved trauma, and rebuild what was broken without the use of drugs and alcohol. So, no matter where you are on your path to recovery, or how many relapses you have had, you can start writing your life story in a different direction today. The difference this time is that you have the advice and tools you need to make it work in your favor. Even if you have relapses on your course, you know now how to stick with your plan and keep your progress toward a happier, more fulfilling life.

About the Author

Evie Wright struggled with her drinking from an early age. By the time she was a teenager, she was using drugs as well. She tried to stop several times without any real success. After being sexually assaulted by a colleague when Evie was in her early twenties, she felt broken, and she started having flashbacks of the traumas caused by her authoritative father as a young child. It was a turning point as she finally figured out that her complex childhood trauma was the very reason behind her drinking. She was referred to two different therapists, one would help her work on her trauma and another helped with her addiction. It was hard to juggle both and to integrate the two treatments herself. This was when she found the special association she's a member of. Its goal is to help people who, just like her, suffered from both childhood traumas and substance dependence. For the first time, she was able to address both problems at once, which allowed her to make a recovery she could sustain.

Evie finally found a sense of resilience, peace, and purpose. Her life changed for the better at all levels, and she became capable of building healthier relationships with her husband and children. But most importantly, she started helping the newcomers in her association to make the change they needed to save their lives. Helping others gain recovery skills and overcome their relapses was a source of great joy to her and helped her maintain her own progress as well. After pursuing this commitment for years, and witnessing the great power of the recovery programs she helped others tailor for themselves, she set her mind to help even more people outside her community.

Today, Evie Wright is proud of her accomplishments in her recovery journey. She is also a proud military veteran, wife, and mother of two children. She is still very active in her efforts with a local association that helps addicts with PTSD.

References

Albert Jay Nock. (1940). *Meditations in Wall Street.* New York, W. Morrow & Co.

American Psychiatric Association. (2017). *Diagnostic and statistical manual of mental disorders: DSM-5.* CBS Publishers & Distributors, Pvt. Ltd.

American Psychological Association. (2010). *Psychodynamic Psychotherapy Brings Lasting Benefits through Self-Knowledge.* Https://Www.apa.org. https://www.apa.org/news/press/releases/2010/01/psychodynamic-therapy

BetterHealth Australia. (2020). *Trauma and children—newborns to two years.* Better Health Channel. https://www.betterhealth.vic.gov.au/health/healthyliving/trauma-and-children-newborns-to-two-years#common-reactions-to-trauma-in-babies-and-toddlers

Black Bear Lodge. (2021). *The stages of PTSD recovery.* https://blackbearrehab.com/mental-health/ptsd/the-stages-of-ptsd-recovery/

BrainLine. (2018, February 22). *DSM-5 criteria for PTSD.* https://www.brainline.org/article/dsm-5-criteria-ptsd?gclid=CjwKCAjwhOyJBhA4EiwAEcJdcQnabVrml0Fq4JT98kLJfY0CXiU5sfnJ2iwbW20R9EcOBEpQF9P2XRoCcUIQAvD_BwE

Branden, N. (1994). *The six pillars of self-esteem.* Bantam.

Budenz, A., Klein, A., & Prutzman, Y. (2021). The relationship between trauma exposure and adult tobacco use: analysis of the National Epidemiologic Survey on Alcohol and Related

Conditions (III). *Nicotine & Tobacco Research*, *23*(10). https://doi.org/10.1093/ntr/ntab057

Burning Tree Ranch in Addiction. (2019, November 8). *Treating addiction as a symptom of trauma.* https://www.burningtreeranch.com/treating-addiction-as-a-symptom-of-trauma/

Capurso, N. A., & Ross, D. A. (2017). As hopes have flown before: toward the rational design of treatments for Alcohol Use Disorder. *Biological Psychiatry*, *81*(11), e79–e81. https://doi.org/10.1016/j.biopsych.2017.03.016

Carruth, B. (2006). Psychological trauma and addiction treatment. *Journal of Chemical Dependency Treatment*, *8*(2), 1–14. https://doi.org/10.1300/j034v08n02_01

CDC. (2021, March 5). *Preventing teen dating violence.* Center for Disease Control and Prevention. https://www.cdc.gov/violenceprevention/intimatepartnerviolence/teendatingviolence/fastfact.html

Creek, A. (2021). *The Way Out: Ashley Creek's Story about Childhood Trauma and Substance Use.* Cardinal Innovations. https://www.cardinalinnovations.org/Resources/Blog/The-Way-Out-Ashley-Creek-s-Story-about-Childhood-Trauma-and-Substance-Use

Early Connections. (n.d.). *Trauma-informed care.* https://earlyconnections.mo.gov/professionals/trauma-informed-care

Federation of Families for Children's Mental Health, & NCTSN. (2003). What is child traumatic stress? *Claiming Children.* NCTSN. https://www.nctsn.org/resources/what-child-traumatic-stress

Freud, S., & Phillips, A. (2005). *On murder, mourning and melancholia.* Penguin.

Gabor Maté. (2018). *In the realm of hungry ghosts: close encounters with addiction*. Vintage Canada.

Gallagher, W. (2017, December 11). *Your recovery story: how and why you should share it*. Black Bear Lodge. https://blackbearrehab.com/blog/recovery-story-share/

Gladwell, M. (2013). *David and Goliath: underdogs, misfits, and the art of battling giants*. Little, Brown And Company.

Hackensack Meridian Carrier Clinic. (2019, August 6). *Trauma and Addiction*. https://carrierclinic.org/2019/08/06/trauma-and-addiction/

Healthwise. (2020, September 23). *PTSD and suicide thoughts*. University of Michigan Health. https://www.uofmhealth.org/health-library/ad1034spec

Heffernan, K., Cloitre, M., Tardiff, K., Marzuk, P. M., Portera, L., & Leon, A. C. (2000). Childhood trauma as a correlate of lifetime opiate use in psychiatric patients. *Addictive Behaviors, 25*(5), 797–803. https://doi.org/10.1016/s0306-4603(00)00066-6

High Focus Centers. (2021). *Types of trauma disorders*. https://highfocuscenters.pyramidhealthcarepa.com/about/education-center/trauma-disorders/

Jacobsen, L. K., Southwick, S. M., & Kosten, T. R. (2001). Substance use disorders in patients with posttraumatic stress disorder: a review of the literature. *The American Journal of Psychiatry, 158*(8), 1184–1190. https://doi.org/10.1176/appi.ajp.158.8.1184

Juergens, J. (2017). *12 step programs for addiction recovery*. Addiction Center. https://www.addictioncenter.com/treatment/12-step-programs/

Kaimal, G., Ray, K., & Muniz, J. (2016). Reduction of cortisol levels and participants' responses following art making. *Art Therapy, 33*(2), 74–80. https://doi.org/10.1080/07421656.2016.1166832

Khoury, L., Tang, Y. L., Bradley, B., Cubells, J. F., & Ressler, K. J. (2010). Substance use, childhood traumatic experience, and Posttraumatic Stress Disorder in an urban civilian population. *Depression and Anxiety*, *27*(12), 1077–1086. https://doi.org/10.1002/da.20751

Lesser, B. (2021, March 16). *The Unfortunate Connection between childhood trauma and addiction in adulthood.* Dual Diagnosis. https://dualdiagnosis.org/unfortunate-connection-childhood-trauma-addiction-adulthood/

Najavits, L. M. (2019). *Finding your best self: recovery from addiction, trauma, or both* (pp.1–8, 183–186). The Guilford Press.

New Method Wellness. (2017, May 3). *Art therapy for treating substance abuse and dual diagnosis.* https://www.newmethodwellness.com/treatment-methods/art-therapy/

Ouimette, P. C., Brown, P. J., & Najavits, L. M. (1998). Course and treatment of patients with both substance use and posttraumatic stress disorders. *Addictive Behaviors*, *23*(6), 785–795. https://doi.org/10.1016/s0306-4603(98)00064-1

Ouimette, P., Read, J. P., & American Psychological Association. (2014). *Trauma and substance abuse: causes, consequences, and treatment of comorbid disorders* (pp. 95–114, 253–279). American Psychological Association.

P, J. (2019). My recovery discovery. *Here to Help*, *15*(2). https://www.heretohelp.bc.ca/visions/blips-and-dips-vol15/my-recovery-discovery

Pena, B. (2014, December 5). *Inspirational recovery story—Matt S.* Addiction Hope. https://www.addictionhope.com/recovery/inspirational-stories/inspirational-recovery-story-matt-s/

Peterson, S. (2018a, March 23). *How early childhood trauma is unique.* The National Child Traumatic Stress Network.

https://www.nctsn.org/what-is-child-trauma/trauma-types/early-childhood-trauma/effects

Peterson, S. (2018b, November 5). *About child trauma.* The National Child Traumatic Stress Network. https://www.nctsn.org/what-is-child-trauma/about-child-trauma

Shaili Jain. (2019). *The unspeakable mind: stories of trauma and healing from the frontlines of PTSD science.* Harper.

Silver Mist Recovery. (2018, September 11). *The link between childhood trauma and addiction in adulthood.* https://silvermistrecovery.com/blog/2018/09/2019-guide-the-link-between-childhood-trauma-and/

Staff, O. T. R. (2020, January 16). *Stories: trauma and addiction.* Oregon Trail Recovery. https://oregontrailrecovery.com/blog/stories-trauma-and-addiction/

White, L. (2021, October 1). *From deadly cocaine addiction to happiness and health.* Detox to Rehab. https://detoxtorehab.com/true-stories-of-addiction/deadly-cocaine-addiction-happiness-health

Youell, J. (2021, September 20). *Understanding regression psychology.* Better Help. https://www.betterhelp.com/advice/psychologists/understanding-regression-psychology/

Made in United States
Troutdale, OR
02/18/2024